PRAISE FOR *INSPIRED*

"Besides being such an intelligent, often whimsical teacher on something as complicated as the Bible, perhaps the best endorsement I can give Rachel's book *Inspired* is that before I was even halfway through, I told my teenagers I wanted to read it with them. This is the Jesus and the Scriptures I want them to love. This is a brilliant, beautiful offering."

—Jen Hatmaker, author of *New York Times*
bestsellers *Of Mess and Moxie* and *For the Love*

"Rachel Held Evans models a spiritual journey that many are yearning to take: growing into adult readers of the Bible without feeling as though they are leaving the faith of their youth in the process. With her characteristic honesty and warmth, Rachel gives many the language and permission they desperately need to leave behind their guilt and fear, and to read the Bible anew with the joyful anticipation the sacred book deserves."

—Peter Enns, author of *The Bible Tells Me So*

"Rachel Held Evans has taken the stodgy, ancient bundle of work we call the Bible and makes it accessible without trampling its ancient origins or cultural contexts. In doing so, she subverts the strange, modern assumptions we too often bring to its pages. *Inspired* is both delightful and essential."

—Mike McHargue, cofounder of *The
Liturgists*, host of *Ask Science Mike*, and
author of *Finding God in the Waves*

"*Inspired* is a love letter to scripture. Evans takes what has been weaponized against so many of us and she beats it into a ploughshare. She shows us how to love the Bible; how to see its flaws, beauty, strength, and spirit at the same time. That's love. Not worship. Love. I'm so grateful for this expertly written, timely book."

—Nadia Bolz-Weber, pastor and author
of *Pastrix* and *Accidental Saints*

INSPIRED

INSPIRED

SLAYING GIANTS,
WALKING ON WATER,
AND LOVING THE BIBLE AGAIN

RACHEL HELD EVANS

NELSON
BOOKS

An Imprint of Thomas Nelson

Published in Nashville, Tennessee, by Nelson Books, an imprint of Thomas Nelson. Nelson Books and Thomas Nelson are registered trademarks of HarperCollins Christian Publishing, Inc.

Published in association with the Books & Such Literary Agency, 52 Missions Circle, Suite 122, PMB 170, Santa Rosa, CA 95409-5370, www.booksandsuch.biz.

Thomas Nelson titles may be purchased in bulk for educational, business, fund-raising, or sales promotional use. For information, please e-mail SpecialMarkets@ThomasNelson.com.

Unless otherwise noted, Scripture quotations are taken from the Holy Bible, New International Version®, NIV®. Copyright © 1973, 1978, 1984, 2011 by Biblica, Inc.® Used by permission of Zondervan. All rights reserved worldwide. www.Zondervan.com. The "NIV" and "New International Version" are trademarks registered in the United States Patent and Trademark Office by Biblica, Inc.®

Scripture quotations marked ESV are from the ESV® Bible (The Holy Bible, English Standard Version®). Copyright © 2001 by Crossway, a publishing ministry of Good News Publishers. Used by permission. All rights reserved.

Scripture quotations marked NASB are from New American Standard Bible®. Copyright © 1960, 1962, 1963, 1968, 1971, 1972, 1973, 1975, 1977, 1995 by The Lockman Foundation. Used by permission. (www.Lockman.org)

Scripture quotations marked NRSV are from New Revised Standard Version Bible. Copyright © 1989 National Council of the Churches of Christ in the United States of America. Used by permission. All rights reserved.

Scripture quotations marked HCSB are from the Holman Christian Standard Bible®, copyright © 1999, 2000, 2002, 2003, 2009 by Holman Bible Publishers. Used by permission. HCSB® is a federally registered trademark of Holman Bible Publishers.

Scripture quotations marked KJV are from the King James Version of the Bible.

ISBN 978-0-7180-2231-0
ISBN 978-0-7180-2232-7 (eBook)
ISBN 978-1-4002-1107-4 (Custom)

Library of Congress Control Number: 2017963332

Printed in the United States of America

19 20 21 22 LSC 10 9 8 7

For my mother-in-law, Norma Evans

Did he believe that God wrote stories with only one kind of meaning? It seemed to me that a story that had only one kind of meaning was not very interesting or worth remembering for too long.

—CHAIM POTOK, *DAVITA'S HARP*

CONTENTS

CONTENTS

INTRODUCTION

"ONCE UPON A TIME . . ."

Once upon a time, there lived a girl with a magic book.
Like many other books, this one told tales of kings and queens, farmers and warriors, giants and sea monsters, and dangerous voyages. But unlike any other, it cast a spell over all who read it so they were pulled into the story, cast as characters in a great epic full of danger and surprise. From the book the girl learned how to be brave like the shepherd boy David, clever like the poor peasant Ruth, and charming like the beautiful queen Esther. She memorized the book's proverbs, which were said to hold the secret to a rich and happy life, and she sang the book's ancient songs, just as they'd been sung for thousands of years. She learned that with enough faith, you could topple a giant with a slingshot, turn water into wine, and survive three days in the belly of a great fish. You could even wrestle an angel. She learned, too, how to defend the book against its enemies, those who said its story wasn't true. She could fashion the book into a weapon if she wanted, and wield its truth like a sword. Rumor had

it the book was divinely inspired, and she believed it, for every word she read echoed with the voice of God.

When the girl met a teacher named Jesus in the story, she heard that voice even louder than before, so she promised to love and follow him forever. Jesus taught her to care for the poor, be kind to the lonely, forgive the bullies, and listen to her mother. He healed the sick and raised the dead and said those who followed him would do the same. The girl never healed the sick or raised the dead, but still she believed.

Then, one day, the story began to unravel. The girl was older now, with a mature and curious mind, and she noticed some things she hadn't before. Like how God rewarded the chosen patriarch Abraham for obeying God's request that he sacrifice his own son. Or how God permitted the chosen people of Israel to kidnap women and girls as spoils of war. After the famous walls of Jericho came a-tumblin' down, a God-appointed army slaughtered every man, woman, and child in the city, and after Pharaoh refused to release his slaves, a God-appointed angel killed every firstborn boy in Egypt. Even the story of all the earth's animals taking refuge in a giant ark, once one of the girl's favorites, began with a God so sorry for creating life, he simply washed it all away. If God was supposed to be the hero of the story, then why did God behave like a villain? If the book was supposed to explain all the mysteries of life, why did it leave her with so many questions?

Deep down she knew there was no such thing as crafty serpents and talking donkeys, and that you could never fit every kind of animal on earth on a boat. Science proves the earth wasn't made in seven days, nor is it held up by "great pillars" as the book claimed. There were contradictions in the various accounts of King David's reign, and even the stories of Jesus' famous resurrection didn't read like reliable newspaper reports.

Perhaps, the girl reasoned, the story wasn't true after all. Perhaps, she feared, her book wasn't magic.

With each question, the voice of God grew quieter and the voices of others grew louder. These were dangerous questions, they said—forbidden questions, especially for a girl. They told her to fight against her doubts, but her sword grew heavy. They told her to stand strong in her faith, but her legs grew weak. Words that once teemed with life nettled her mind, and stories that once captured her imagination triggered her doubts and darkest fears. It was as if the roots of beloved and familiar trees had risen up to trip her on the path. There was no map for a world suddenly rearranged, no incantation to light the road ahead.

She was lost.

And yet the spell remained unbroken. The characters, many more sinister now, wandered in and out of her life just as before, interrupting her work, her relationships, her plans. Old stories continued to be told. Old battles continued to be waged. She couldn't get the ancient songs out of her head.

She was still caught in the story. Like millions before her and millions after, she couldn't run away. In her unguarded moments, she found herself wondering, *Is the magic of the book really divine blessing, or is it, in truth, a curse?*

And that's when the adventure really began.

⁓

Controversial. Sacred. Irrelevant. Timeless. Oppressive. Embattled. Divine.

The Bible conjures all sorts of adjectives among modern-day readers, and yet its "magic" is indisputable, for every time we tease about "forbidden fruit" or praise a good Samaritan, we betray our fascination with this ancient collection of stories and poems, prophecies and proverbs, letters and laws, written and compiled by countless authors spanning multiple centuries and cited by everyone from William Blake to Beyoncé. The Bible has been translated into more than two thousand languages, its tales inspiring the art of Shakespeare and Steinbeck, Zora Neale Hurston and Blind Willie Johnson. Its words are etched into our gravestones, scribbled onto the white posters we carry into picket lines, and strategically incorporated into our dating profiles.

Civil rights activists quoted heavily from biblical texts, as did the Christian segregationists who opposed them. The Bible's ancient refrains have given voice to the laments of millions of oppressed people and, too often, provided justification to their oppressors. Wars still rage over its disputed geographies.

Like it or not, the Bible has cast its spell, and we are caught up in the story.

My own life got grafted in the moment I first drew breath at Saint Vincent's Hospital in Birmingham, Alabama, and was named *Rachel*. In Scripture she is the beautiful shepherdess who stole Jacob's heart, defied her father, nursed a bitter rivalry with her sister, and begged God to give her children right up until the birth of her second took her life. In Birmingham, Alabama, in the hairspray haze of the Reagan era, this Rachel was an intense and imaginative kid with severe eczema, knock-off Keds, and political opinions. When I first learned in Sunday school, at age seven, that my biblical name means *ewe*, I came home crying, certain my parents had taken one look at my naked baby body and declared it *gross*. Learning a *ewe* is simply a female sheep did little to cheer me, especially when my friend Sarah's name meant *princess*.

As a child, I imbibed the stories of Scripture as a fish imbibes the sea. The evangelical subculture of the eighties and nineties produced no shortage of Bible-themed books and videos, so along with the cast of *Sesame Street* and a relentless cavalcade of Disney princesses, the figures of Moses, Miriam, Abraham, and Isaac marched through my imagination. My first Bible was one of those Precious Moments volumes that boasted blond, doe-eyed David on the cover, two baby lambs resting in his arms, and a sparrow perched on his staff, the shepherd boy blissfully unaware that in a few short years he'd be delivering two hundred Philistine foreskins to his father-in-law as a bride price. Inside were all my favorite biblical heroes and heroines depicted as children. (Well, almost all of them. The artists failed to include Jael, whose precious moment involved assassinating a general by driving a tent peg through his skull.) These characters occupied a similar space in my brain as Abraham Lincoln, Bear Bryant, and dead relatives whose antics were conjured up at family gatherings from time to time. They were mythic yet real; true yet more than true. The Bible's stories were the ones in which every other story belonged, the moral universe through which all of life's dramas moved. So convinced was I that I inhabited the same reality as Lot's wife, I refused for years to look out the rear window of our Chevy Caprice for fear of turning into a pillar of salt.

By the time my family relocated to one of the most famous notches of the Bible Belt—Dayton, Tennessee, home of the famous Scopes Monkey Trial of 1925—my evangelical roots ensured I drank deep from the waters of Scripture. I'd memorized large portions of Psalms, Proverbs, and Romans before entering high school, where I served as president of the Bible Club and a leader in my church youth group. (You know you've found your place in the world when you make it to the homecoming court . . . representing the Bible Club.) The pages of my *Ryrie Study Bible* bled yellow, orange, and green from highlighting, and I never missed my morning "quiet time" in the Word. If the Bible of my childhood functioned primarily as a storybook, then the Bible of my adolescence functioned as a hand-book, useful because it told me what to do. I turned to it whenever I had a question about friendships, dating, school, body image, friendship, or any number of adolescent concerns, and it never failed to provide me with a sense of security and direction.

Every evangelical teenager was expected to choose a life verse, and mine was Philippians 3:8: "I count all things to be loss in view of the surpassing value of knowing Christ Jesus my Lord, for whom I have suffered the loss of all things, and count them but rubbish so that I may gain Christ" (NASB). (It's funny now to think that the words in a two-thousand-year-old letter from an imprisoned ex-Pharisee to the members of an obscure religious sect convinced a sixteen-year-old girl in 1997 to choose going to a Bible study over seeing *Titanic* in the theater, but such is the strange power of our biblical text.)

No one was surprised when, after graduating from high school, I enrolled in the English literature program at a conservative Christian college that promised to teach every discipline—from psychology, to history, to economics—from a "biblical worldview perspective." If the Bible of my childhood functioned as a story-book and the Bible of my adolescence a handbook, then the Bible of my young adulthood functioned as an answer book, or position paper, useful because it was *right*. The Bible, I learned, was the reason Christians voted for Republicans, rejected evolution, and opposed same-sex marriage. It was the reason I could never, as a woman, be a pastor, the reason I should always, as a woman, mind my neckline. A biblical worldview, my professors assured me, would prepare me to debate atheists and agnostics, and would equip me to engage the moral confusion of postmodern culture still reeling from September 11, 2001. The more I learned about Scripture, they said, the more confident I would grow in my faith and the better I would be at answering the world's questions.

But their assurances, however sincerely intended, proved empty when, as a young adult, I started asking those questions for myself. Positions I'd been told were clearly "biblical"—young earth creationism, restrictions on women's roles in the home and church, the certainty of hell for all nonbelievers—grew muddier in the midst of lived experience, and the more time I spent seeking clarity from Scripture, the more problems I uncovered. For example, why did my church appeal to Paul's letter to Timothy to oppose women preaching from the pulpit, but ignore his instructions to the Corinthians regarding women covering their heads (1 Timothy 2:12; 1 Corinthians 11:6)? How could we insist the Bible is morally superior to every other religious text when the book of Deuteronomy calls for stoning rebellious children, committing genocide against enemies, and enslaving women captured in war (Deuteronomy 20:14–17; 21:18–21)? What business do I have describing as "inerrant" and "infallible" a text that presumes a flat and stationary earth, takes slavery for granted, and presupposes patriarchal norms like polygamy?

It was as if the Bible had turned into an unsettling version of one of those children's peekaboo books. Beneath the colorful illustration of Noah's ark was—surprise!—the violent destruction of humanity. Turn the page to Joshua and the battle of Jericho and—peekaboo!— it's genocide. Open to Queen Esther's castle and—look!—there's a harem full of concubines. Gone was the comforting storybook of my childhood, the useful handbook of my adolescence, and the definitive answer book of my college years. The Bible of my twenties served only as a stumbling block, a massive obstacle between me and the God I thought I knew.

My parents responded to my questions with compassion, but the evangelical community around me treated them like a wildfire in need of containment. Friends, professors, and Sunday school teachers rushed to offer explanations, often referring me to Gleason Archer's massive *Encyclopedia of Bible Difficulties*, a five-hundred-page tome that promised answers to all the Bible's most challenging puzzles, but which proved less than helpful to a reluctant skeptic previously unaware half of those puzzles existed in the first place. The harder my fellow Christians worked to minimize my objections, the more pronounced those objections became. Beneath all the elaborate justifications for Israel's ethnic cleansing, all the strange theories for where Cain got his wife and how Judas managed to die in two different ways (he hanged himself and *then* fell headlong onto the ground), I sensed a deep insecurity. There was a move-along-nothing-to-see-here quality to their arguments that only reinforced my suspicion that maybe the Bible wasn't magic after all, and maybe, deep down, they knew it. Instead of bolstering my confidence in the Bible, its most strident defenders inadvertently weakened it. Then when a pastor friend asked me what personal sins might have triggered my questions—*"sexual immorality, perhaps?"*—I saw that my journey through these doubts would be a lonely one.

I would leave my faith a dozen times in the years following, only to return to it a dozen more. I got married, became Episcopalian, voted for Barack Obama, and discovered the historical-critical method of biblical interpretation. Armed with a library card and a blog, I delighted in informing people whose life verse was Jeremiah 29:11 ("'For I know the plans I have for you,' declares the LORD, 'plans to prosper you and not to harm you, plans to give you hope and a future'") that those words were directed at the nation of Israel during the Babylonian exile, *not* high school seniors, and I made sure to interrupt references to the Bible's epistles with the knowing caveat, "*if* Paul authored the letter to the Colossians," to the wry chuckles of other readers in the know.

In short, I became something of a Bible bully.

While the scholarship I'd encountered was sound, I used it to render the Bible into little more than a curiosity, an interesting religious artifact to study for sport. Beneath the incessant hum of objections, corrections, and clarifications lay a terrible silence wherein the Bible still fascinated me but no longer spoke to me, at least not with the voice of God. The Bible remained a stumbling block, but a fixture now cold and mute.

My journey back to loving the Bible, like most journeys of faith, is a meandering and ongoing one, a story still in draft. And like all pilgrims, I am indebted to those who have gone before me, those saints of holy curiosity whose lives of faithful questioning taught me not to fear my doubts, but to embrace and learn from them.

Memoirist Addie Zierman writes an online advice column, "Dear Addie," for people who have left legalistic religious backgrounds. Recently a reader named Megan asked for advice on how to engage the Bible when it comes with so much baggage, when it tends to trigger more doubts than it resolves. Zierman advised Megan to think of the Bible not as one of those *Magic Eye* books, which, with enough squinting and studying, reveal a single hidden image, but rather as a song that can be covered and remixed by a variety of artists. "Find your cover artists," she wrote. "Find the voices that help you hear the same songs differently."[1]

Over the course of the last decade, I have discovered my cover artists—those scholars and poets, traditions and practices, that help make the Bible sing. From the rich history of Jewish interpretation, I learned the mysteries and contradictions of Scripture weren't meant to be fought against, but courageously engaged, and that the Bible by its very nature invites us to wrestle, doubt, imagine, and debate. Liberation theology (which views the Bible through the lens of becoming free from unjust conditions) and feminist biblical interpretations showed me how the stories of Scripture could be wisely appropriated for social good by pointing us to justice. The spiritual practices of *Lectio Divina* and Ignatian meditation, which invite contemplative engagement with the text, helped me recover a devotional element to Scripture reading that had long ago gone missing.

Through their faithful example, my parents continue to remind me the whole purpose of biblical devotion is to be "thoroughly equipped for every good work" (2 Timothy 3:17); and Old Testament scholar Peter Enns, whom I count as both a mentor and friend, has encouraged me to approach Scripture with a new set of questions, questions like, "What if the Bible is just fine the way it is? . . . Not the well-behaved-everything-is-in-order version we create, but the messy, troubling, weird, and ancient Bible that we actually have?"[2]

These questions loosened my grip on the text and gave me permission to love the Bible for what it is, not what I want it to be. And here's the surprising thing about that. When you stop trying to force the Bible to be something it's not—static, perspicacious, certain, absolute—then you're free to revel in what it is: living, breathing, confounding, surprising, and yes, perhaps even magic. The ancient rabbis likened Scripture to a palace, alive and bustling, full of grand halls, banquet rooms, secret passages, and locked doors.

"The adventure," wrote Rabbi Burton L. Visotzky in *Reading the Book*, lies in "learning the secrets of the palace, unlocking all the doors and perhaps catching a glimpse of the King in all His splendor."[3]

Renowned New Testament scholar N. T. Wright compared Scripture to a five-act play, full of drama and surprise, wherein the people of God are invited into the story to improvise the unfinished, final act.[4] Our ability to faithfully execute our roles in the drama depends on our willingness to enter the narrative, he said, to see how our own stories intersect with the grander epic of God's redemption of the world. Every page of Scripture serves as an invitation—to wonder, to wrestle, to surrender to the adventure.

And so, at thirty-five, after years of tangling with the Bible, and with every expectation that I shall tangle with it forever, I find myself singing Psalm 121 to my baby boy each night. *"He who watches over you will not slumber,"* I sing into his sweet-smelling wisp of hair, as many thousands of mothers and fathers have done before. *"He who watches over Israel will neither slumber nor sleep."*

I am teaching my son the ancient songs and hearing them again for the first time. I am caught up in the story, surrendered to its pull.

Citing G. K. Chesterton, author Neil Gaiman often noted, "Fairy tales are more than true—not because they tell us that dragons exist, but because they tell us that dragons can be beaten."[5] In those first, formative years of my life, before I knew or cared about culture wars or genre categories or biblical interpretation, this is what Scripture taught me: that a boat full of animals can survive a catastrophic flood, that seas can be parted and lions tamed, that girls can be prophets and warriors and queens, that a kid's lunch of fish and bread can be multiplied to feed five thousand people.

At times I wonder if I understood my sacred text better then than I do now or ever will again.

My aim with this book is to recapture some of that Bible magic, but in a way that honors the text for what it is—ancient, complicated, debated, and untidy, both universally relevant and born from a specific context and culture. I write with two audiences in mind: first, those who share my evangelical background and find themselves navigating the great chasm between Scripture as they learned it and Scripture as what it actually is, and second, those who share my present affiliation with progressive mainline traditions and are itching to explore more deeply the background, significance, and relevance of the texts sampled in the liturgy each week. I hope to show how the Bible can be captivating and true when taken on its own terms, avoiding both strict literalism on the one hand and safe, disinterested liberalism on the other.

I've arranged the book around various biblical genres, alternating between short, creative retellings of familiar Bible stories ("The Temple," "The Well," "The Walls," and so on), and more in-depth explorations of those genres ("Origin Stories," "Deliverance Stories," "War Stories," and so forth). Woven throughout are reflections from my own life and invitations for readers to consider how their stories intersect with those of the Bible.

I tackle this subject not as a scholar, but as a storyteller and literature lover who believes understanding the genre of a given text is the first step to engaging it in a meaningful way. My focus is on the Bible as a collection of stories, stories best able to teach us when we appreciate their purpose. For the scholarship, I rely heavily on the work of Peter Enns, as well as the writings of Walter Brueggemann, Ellen Davis, Delores Williams, Nyasha Junior, Amy-Jill Levine, Soong-Chan Rah, J. R. Daniel Kirk, Scot McKnight, Glenn R. Paauw, and N. T. Wright. I'm more grateful than ever for the faithful contributions of these fellow pilgrims.

A book about the Bible by a memoirist may seem like an odd undertaking, but anyone who has loved the Bible as much as I have, and who has lost it and found it again, knows how a relationship with the Bible can be as real and as complicated as a relationship with a family member or close friend. For better or worse, my story is inextricably tethered to the stories of Scripture, right down to my first name. Rather than attempting to rend the threads of my life from those of the sacred text, I hope to better understand their interconnectedness and, perhaps, to step back far enough to see a tapestry emerge.

The Bible never refers to sacred Scripture as "magic," which is understandable since the term carried even more cultic baggage in the ancient world than it does today. Instead, the author of 2 Timothy 3:16 declares, "All Scripture is inspired by God" (NASB). Here the writer has created a new word—*theopneustos*—a combination of the Greek *theo,* meaning "god," and *pneo,* meaning "to breathe out" or "to blow." *Inspiration,* both in the English language and in its ancestral languages, is rooted in the imagery of divine breath, the eternal rhythm of inhale and exhale, gather and release. The book of John describes the breath of God as blowing wherever it pleases. "You hear its sound," the text says, "but you cannot tell where it comes from or where it is going" (3:8). It's the invisible power of wind in sails, the strange alchemy of air on embers. You couldn't track it down even if you tried.

Inspiration is better than magic, for as any artist will tell you, true inspiration comes not to the lucky or the charmed but to the faithful—to the writer who shows up at her keyboard each morning, even when she's far too tired, to the guitarist whose fingers bleed after hours of practice, to the dancer who must first learn the traditional steps before she can freestyle with integrity. Inspiration is not about some disembodied ethereal voice dictating words or notes to a catatonic host. It's a collaborative process, a holy give-and-take, a partnership between Creator and creator.

While Christians believe the Bible to be uniquely revelatory and authoritative to the faith, we have no reason to think its many authors were exempt from the mistakes, edits, rewrites, and dry spells of everyday creative work. Nor should we, as readers, expect every encounter with the text to leave us happily awestruck and enlightened. Inspiration, on both the giving and receiving end, takes practice and patience. It means showing up even when you don't feel like it, even when it seems as if no one else is there. It means waiting for wind to stir.

God is still breathing. The Bible is both inspired and inspiring.

Our job is to ready the sails and gather the embers, to discuss and debate, and like the biblical character Jacob, to wrestle with the mystery until God gives us a blessing.

If you're curious, you will never leave the text without learning something new. If you're persistent, you just might leave inspired.

THE TEMPLE

Where is your brother?"

Even in the soft glow of the lamplight, Mama's features look worn with worry. The challah has been baked, prayers have been said, and Papa has put down his tools and is bouncing little Hanan on his knee. Sabbath has officially begun, with or without Hannah's delinquent younger brother.

She'd done her best to track him down. As the sun receded over the vast Babylonian territory, she ran up and down the river Chebar, shouting Haggai's name and knocking on nearly every door of their dusty little town known as *Al-Yahudu*, "the village of the Jews."[1]

"He knows the way home," Hannah says, the familiar scents of home soothing her into blithe resignation. "He's not a baby anymore, Mama. He'll be an archer in the army in just two or three years."

Mama mutters something under her breath about cold desert nights and loose Babylonian women.

Not two minutes after Hannah collapses at Papa's feet, eager for another of his evening stories, Haggai bursts through the front door like a hungry puppy.

"Sorry I'm late!" he shouts, breathless. "I was in the city."

"Just as I'd feared," Mama says.

Haggai moves with the restless energy of someone with news, someone with a story to tell.

"They were celebrating the Akitu festival," he says. "You wouldn't believe all the food and drink! Women everywhere were dancing. They gave me figs and olives. And they told the most amazing story, Papa, the story of how Marduk became the most supreme god and established his throne in the great temple."

Mama and Papa exchange looks.

Haggai, paying no mind to the tension in the room, straightens up, clears his throat, and with the authority of a wizened elder, relates to them the tale:

"In the beginning, before the heaven and earth were named, there lived two wild and capricious gods: Tiamat, goddess of salt water, and Apsu, god of freshwater. These two gods mingled together to produce many other gods, filling the whole cosmos with clamor and chaos. Nothing was in its right place.

"When the younger gods grew so noisy that Apsu couldn't sleep, he resolved to kill each one of them. A battle ensued, but instead of quieting the noise, Apsu faltered and was killed by Ea, father of the great Marduk.

"Enraged, Tiamat advanced on Marduk and his forces, backed by a massive army of demons and monsters, hurricanes and hounds.

"But Marduk was a valiant warrior, so he challenged his great-great grandmother to do battle alone with him. The two fought and fought until Marduk captured Tiamat in a net and drove a great wind into her mouth so that she became bloated and slow. Marduk shot an arrow into Tiamat's belly, cutting through her insides and puncturing her heart. Then he split her body into two pieces, flinging half of the corpse into the heavens to hold back the waters behind the firmament, and the other half to the earth to hold back the waters that rage below. From her hollowed eyes flowed the Tigris and Euphrates Rivers.

"Then Marduk made the stars and moon and assigned the gods to various duties. He put everything in order—sky, land, plants, and animals. Among the gods he took the highest place, and from the blood of his enemies he created humanity to serve as their slaves. Finally, Marduk saw that a great temple was made in his honor, a temple from which he could rule and rest.

"He lives in the temple, right here in Babylon, to this day," Haggai concludes. "And the king is his emissary."

Haggai takes a bow.

The house is quiet for a few minutes. Only the crackling fire joins Hanan in his cooing. Mama and Papa look sad.

Finally, after what seems like a very long time, Papa invites the whole family to gather around him. "I have a story too," he says, a twinkle returning to his eye, "one told to me by my father, which was told to him by his father, which was told to him by his father. It is an old story. So listen carefully."

"In the beginning," he says, "before heaven and earth were named, there was *Elohim*—there was God.

"Now the cosmos was formless and void. Nothing was in its right place. But the Spirit of God hovered over the chaotic waters and said, 'Let there be light.' And there was light, and it was good. God separated the light from the dark, calling one *day* and the other *night*. This is what God did on the first day.

"Then God said, 'Let there be water above and water below.' So God made the firmament, a great dome to hold back the waters of the sky, and it, too, was good. God separated the waters, calling all that was above *heaven*, and all that was below *earth*. This is what God did on the second day.

"Then God separated the land from the seas, and God said, 'Let the land produce all kinds of plants—fruit and flowers, wheat and willow trees.' And sure enough, the land sprouted. Grass grew. Grapes ripened. Trees stretched out their arms and dug in their roots. Lilies bloomed. All of this God did on the third day, and it was very, very good.

"On the fourth day, God pinned the lights to the firmament: sun, moon, and stars. 'Let these lights serve as timekeepers,' God said, 'to mark the days and years and special seasons.' And God saw that the lights were good, each one in just the right place, each one with a special assignment.

"Then, on the fifth day, God said, 'Let the waters below teem with living creatures and let birds soar through the sky.' So God stocked the oceans with sharks and eels and seahorses and fish, and God filled the sky with eagles and sparrows and humming-birds and owls. The whole earth was swimming and flying, swarming and soaring, but still it wasn't enough. So on the sixth day, God created all the animals of the land: cattle, camels, sheep, snakes, mighty stags and timid field mice, ferocious lions and wise little ants. And God separated all the creatures into families and said, 'Be fruitful and multiply! Fill up the earth!' But still it wasn't enough.

"So God said, 'Let there be people. And let them rule over my creation as my emissaries, little kings and queens, created in my image and of my nature.' So God made people on the sixth day, and God told them to be fruitful and to multiply, to use all the plants and animals for their good and to be responsible with the world.

"When God reached the seventh day, God saw that creation was in order. Everything was in the right place. The work was finished, and all of it was good. So on the seventh day God rested, which is why we rest today.

"It is a holy day," Papa says, "set apart to remember our good and sovereign God."

Their home is quiet for a moment.

"You mean there was no great battle?" Haggai asks.

"No battle," Papa says.

"No grandmothers getting split in two," Mama adds.

"And all people are God's emissaries, not just the king?" Haggai asks.

"Yes. All people are God's emissaries," Papa says. "We are each created in God's image, charged with watching over creation. We are not slaves, my son."

Haggai thinks for a moment.

"But what about a temple? If Marduk lives in the temple, then where does *Elohim* live? We don't have a temple for him."

Hannah lowers her head to avoid catching her parents' eyes. She knows this is a sensitive subject throughout Al-Yahudu, for once her people boasted a beautiful temple, one renowned throughout the world. But the Babylonians destroyed it. The God of the Jews has no place to live.

But Papa doesn't grimace. Instead, he says, "Ah, that is what makes our God so great, Haggai. Our God doesn't need a temple of stone from which to rule and rest. Our God's home is the whole earth. God rests and rules *everywhere*. There is a song that puts it well. It goes:

"'Heaven is my throne,' says the LORD, 'and the earth is my footstool.

"'Do you think I need a house to be at home? Have I not made everything you see? The whole universe is my abode!

"'The only thing I want,' says the Lord, 'are people with humble and contrite hearts, people who observe my ways. In the presence of those people I will make my home.'"[2]

5

Hannah is surprised to see that Mama is crying. Haggai, too, looks somber.

"I'm sorry I was late for Sabbath prayers," he says.

"It's all right, little king," Papa says, tousling his hair. "God is slow to anger and quick to forgive ... Now, let's get on with supper."

ORIGIN STORIES

Our Bible was forged from a crisis of faith. Though many of its stories, proverbs, and poems were undoubtedly passed down through oral tradition, scholars believe the writing and compilation of most of Hebrew Scripture, also known as the Old Testament, began during the reign of King David and gained momentum during the Babylonian invasion of Judah and in the wake of the Babylonian exile, when Israel was occupied by that mighty pagan empire.

One cannot overstate the trauma of this exile. The people of Israel had once boasted a king, a temple, and a great expanse of land—all of which they believed had been given to them by God and ensured to them forever. But in the sixth century BC, King Nebuchadnezzar laid siege to Jerusalem, destroying both the city and its temple. Many of the Jews who lived there were taken captive and forced into the empire's service. Others remained, but without a king, without a place of worship, without a national identity. This catastrophic event threw everything the people of Israel believed about themselves and about their God into question. Many assumed their collective sins were to blame and that with repentance their honor might be restored. Others feared God had abandoned them completely. Priests wondered how to conduct rituals and sacrifices without a temple or an altar, and parents worried their children would grow enamored by the wealth and power of Babylon and forget their own people's most cherished values.

The words of Psalm 137:1–6 capture the agony:

> By the rivers of Babylon we sat and wept
>> when we remembered Zion.
> There on the poplars
>> we hung our harps,
> for there our captors asked us for songs,
>> our tormentors demanded songs of joy;
> they said, "Sing us one of the songs of Zion!"
>
> How can we sing the songs of the LORD
>> while in a foreign land?
> If I forget you, Jerusalem,
>> may my right hand forget its skill.
> May my tongue cling to the roof of my mouth
>> if I do not remember you,
> if I do not consider Jerusalem
>> my highest joy.

It should come as no surprise to any writer that all this emotional suffering produced some quality literature. Jewish scribes got to work, pulling together centuries of oral and written material and adding reflections of their own as they wrestled through this national crisis of faith. If the people of Israel no longer had their own land, their own king, or their own temple, what *did* they have?

They had their stories. They had their songs. They had their traditions and laws. They had the promise that the God who set all of creation in order, who told Abraham his descendants would outnumber the stars, who rescued the Hebrews from slavery, who spoke to them from Mount Sinai, and who turned a shepherd boy into a king, would remain present with them no matter what. This God would be faithful.

Today we still return to our roots in times of crisis; we look to the stories of our origins to make sense of things, to remember who we are. The role of origin stories, both in the ancient Near Eastern culture from which the Old Testament emerged and at that familiar kitchen table where you first learned the story of how your grandparents met, is to enlighten the present by recalling the past. Origin stories are rarely straightforward history. Over the years, they morph into a colorful amalgam of truth and myth, nostalgia and cautionary tale, the shades of their significance brought out by the particular light of a particular moment.

Contrary to what many of us are told, Israel's origin stories weren't designed to answer scientific, twenty-first-century questions about the beginning of the universe or the biological evolution of human beings, but rather were meant to answer then-pressing, ancient questions about the nature of God and God's relationship to creation. Even the story of Adam and Eve, found in Genesis 2 and 3, is thought by many scholars to be less a story about *human* origins and more a story about *Israel's* origins, a symbolic representation of Israel's pattern of habitation, disobedience, and exile, set in primeval time.[1]

My friend Kerlin, an Episcopal priest with blue hair, once said the thing she loves most about the Bible is that it sweeps her into an epic story in which she is *not* the central character. As much as we may wish them to be, our present squabbles over science, politics, and public school textbooks were not on the minds of those Jewish scribes seeking to assure an oppressed and scattered people they were still beloved by God. To demand that the Bible meet our demands is to put ourselves and our own interests at the center of the story, which is one of the first traps we must learn to avoid if we are to engage the Bible with integrity or care.

Indeed, one cannot seriously engage the origin stories of the Pentateuch—Genesis, Exodus, Leviticus, Numbers, and Deuteronomy—without encountering ancient and foreign assumptions about the nature of reality. The first creation account of Genesis 1, for example, presumes the existence of a firmament, a vast dome into which the stars and moon were affixed, believed by the Hebrews and their ancient neighbors to keep great cascades of water above the earth from crashing into the land below. An entire day is devoted to the creation of this "vault between the waters" (Genesis 1:6), with no mention of the fact that modern science proves no such atmospheric contraption exists.

In addition to sharing a cosmological worldview with their neighbors, the Jewish scribes who compiled the Hebrew Scripture shared literary sensibilities with them. If, like me, you read the *Epic of Gilgamesh* in college, you already know there are striking similarities between that Akkadian poem, which likely predates Genesis, and the story of Noah. Both involve a worldwide flood and a noble character who builds a boat, rescues the earth's animals, releases birds to see if the waters have subsided, and eventually survives when the boat comes to rest on a mountain. Questions regarding which community borrowed from which are less important than simply acknowledging the fact that Israel shared a conceptual world with its neighbors and used similar literary genres and stories to address issues of identity and purpose.

"It is a fundamental misunderstanding of Genesis," wrote Peter Enns, "to expect it to answer questions generated by a modern worldview, such as whether the days were literal or figurative, or whether the days of creation can be lined up with modern science, or whether the flood was local or universal. The question that Genesis is prepared to answer is whether Yahweh, the God of Israel, is worthy of worship."[2]

You don't have to be a biblical scholar to recognize these genre categories for what they are. In the same way we automatically adjust our expectations when a story begins with "Once upon a time" versus "The Associated Press is reporting . . . ," we instinctively sense upon reading the stories of Adam and Eve and Noah's ark that these tales of origin aren't meant to be straightforward recitations of historical fact. The problem isn't that liberal scholars are imposing novel interpretations on our sacred texts; the problem is that over time we've been conditioned to deny our instincts about what kinds of stories we're reading when those stories are found in the Bible. We've been instructed to reject any trace of poetry, myth, hyperbole, or symbolism even when those literary forms are virtually shouting at us from the page via talking snakes and enchanted trees. That's because there's a curious but popular notion circulating around the church these days that says God would never stoop to using ancient genre categories to communicate. Speaking to ancient people using their own language, literary structures, and cosmological assumptions would be beneath God, it is said, for only our modern categories of science and history can convey the truth in any meaningful way.

In addition to once again prioritizing modern, Western (and often uniquely American) concerns, this notion overlooks one of the most central themes of Scripture itself: God stoops. From walking with Adam and Eve through the garden of Eden, to traveling with the liberated Hebrew slaves in a pillar of cloud and fire, to slipping into flesh and eating, laughing, suffering, healing, weeping, and dying among us as part of humanity, the God of Scripture stoops and stoops and stoops and stoops. At the heart of the gospel message is the story of a God who stoops to the point of death on a cross. Dignified or not, believable or not, ours is a God perpetually on bended knee, doing everything it takes to convince stubborn and petulant children that they are seen and loved. It is no more beneath God to speak to us using poetry, proverb, letters, and legend than it is for a mother to read storybooks to her daughter at bedtime. This is who God is. This is what God does.

While the circumstances of the exiled Israelites may seem far removed from us today, the questions raised by that national crisis of faith remain as pressing as ever: Why do bad things happen to good people? Will evil and death continue to prevail? What does it mean to be chosen by God? Is God faithful? Is God present? Is God good?

Rather than answering these questions in propositions, the Spirit spoke the language of stories, quickening the memories of prophets and the pens of scribes to call a lost and searching people to gather together and *remember*:

> *Remember how in the beginning, God put everything in order and made the whole cosmos a temple? Remember how we are created in God's image, as stewards, not slaves? Remember how Adam and Eve disobeyed, how Cain and Abel fought, how all the people of the earth grew so rebellious and cruel that God regretted creating the world in the first place? Remember how one family's faithfulness was enough to save them from the Great Flood?*
>
> *Remember how God promised an elderly Abraham his descendants would outnumber the stars? Remember how Sarah laughed? Remember how God chose a peopleless nomad, a*

second-born son, a stuttering runaway, and a little shepherd boy to create, liberate, and rule a nation? Remember how that nation is named for a man who limped from wrestling with God?

Remember how God saw the suffering of the banished Hagar, the unloved Leah, and the oppressed Hebrew slaves? Remember how Pharaoh's mighty army drowned in the sea?

Remember the desert? Remember the manna? Remember the water from rock?

Remember how it is our God who said, "Do not fear, for I have redeemed you; I have called you by name, you are mine" (Isaiah 43:1 NRSV)?

Remember how this God has been faithful?

This collective remembering produced the Bible as we know it and explains why it looks the way it does—foreign yet familiar, sacred yet indelibly smudged with human fingerprints. The Bible's original readers may not share our culture, but they share our humanity, and the God they worshipped invited them to bring that humanity to their theology, prayers, songs, and stories.

And so we have on our hands a Bible that includes psalms of praise but also psalms of complaint and anger, a Bible that poses big questions about the nature of evil and the cause of suffering without always answering them. We have a Bible that says in one place that "with much wisdom comes much sorrow" (Ecclesiastes 1:18) and in another "wisdom is supreme—so get wisdom" (Proverbs 4:7 HCSB). We have a Bible concerned with what to do when your neighbor's donkey falls into a pit and exactly how much cinnamon to add to anointing oil. We have a Bible that depicts God as aloof and in control in one moment, and vulnerable and humanlike in the next, a Bible that has frustrated even the best systematic theologians for centuries because it's a Bible that so rarely behaves.

In short, we have on our hands a Bible as complicated and dynamic as our relationship with God, one that reads less like divine monologue and more like an intimate conversation. Our most sacred stories emerged from a rift in that relationship, an intense crisis of faith. Those of us who spend as much time doubting as we do believing can take enormous comfort in that.

The Bible is for us too.

ᘒ

I come from mountain people. In the shadow of Grandfather Mountain, forty winding miles from the closest city and ensconced in a cold Appalachian holler, lies a graveyard where most of my extended family is buried. The dates on the tombstones stretch back to before the Civil War, and the inscriptions conjure memories of Christmases at my great-grandmother's farmhouse when a baffling mix of aunts and uncles, cousins, and neighbors told stories about my ancestors—Dewy, Buck, Wick, Ethel, Tarp, Cordi, Freddie, and Toots—whose legends were as strange as their names.

Take Uncle Wick and Aunt Ethel, for example. As the story goes, one hot July morning, Uncle Wick and a gaggle of local boys got themselves some discount fireworks from an out-of-towner's tent in Bakersville. Aunt Ethel did not approve. The daughter of a coal miner, she respected explosives too much to abide anyone horsing around with them, so she told Uncle Wick he'd have to toss all those Roman candles and bottle rockets in the creek if he expected to get any supper that night. But Uncle Wick, being stubborn, and probably a little sexist, waved her off and went about his scheming. That evening, as the moon rose and the drinks flowed, he filled the front lawn with friends and family and put on a fireworks show worthy of the National Mall.

Sure enough, not ten minutes into the revelry, Uncle Wick came charging into the kitchen, a bloody handkerchief pressed to his hand, screaming, "Ethel! Ethel! I done blowed my finger off!"

Without even looking up from her sink of dishes, Aunt Ethel replied, "Well goody, goody."

That response became so enshrined in our family parlance, I heard it every time I fought my mother on wearing a jacket to school only to come home complaining about the cold bus, or looked for sympathy after flunking a test for which I refused to study, or spent a weekend nursing a sunburn, having lied about wearing sunblock. Mom would give me a wry smile and say, "Well goody, goody," just like her mother and her mother's mother before that. I rolled my eyes, but the joke reminded me I belong to a long line of unflappable southern women.

Even my middle name, Grace, harks back to my great-grandmother, a woman whose dry wit charmed all but the crustiest farmhands, and whose picture in the family photo album shows her frowning in front of the smokehouse, holding a hog's head by the ears. Grace was the first woman in Mitchell County to drive a car, and her daughter, my grandmother, was one of the first to go to college. I once scaled a small boulder to get a picture of a dewy leaf for Instagram, so clearly the legacy of valor continues.

Origin stories take all sorts of forms, from the story of why the women of my family say "goody, goody," to the explanation for why there's a rusty toilet seat hanging from your grandfather's barn door, to the legends that urge us to idealize our nation's founders, to the reason your Jewish neighbors dip celery in salt water at their Passover meal each year. So ubiquitous they can blend into the scenery, origin stories permeate our language, our assumptions, our routines.

An eighteenth-century English naval officer once raised a telescope to his blind eye to ensure he'd miss the signal from his superior ordering him to withdraw from battle, and two hundred years later, we still talk about politicians "turning a blind eye" to corruption. My friends and I drink at a place called Monkey Town Brewery because eighty years ago our town prosecuted a substitute teacher for presenting the theory of evolution to a biology class, bringing the "Trial of the Century" to Dayton, Tennessee. The ghosts of old gods haunt our calendars—Thursday marking "Thor's Day"—and the heroes of centuries past still hunt and battle and dance across our night sky. Cultures worldwide treasure their creation myths, those passed-down tales that orient a people in the universe and explain how it all began, whether it was from a lotus risen from the navel of Vishnu (Hindu), or out of the belly of the Rainbow Serpent (Aboriginal), or from the Spider Woman guiding the lost to a new world (Hopi). Americans love stories about billion-dollar companies that started in garages and superheroes bitten by radioactive insects.

Origin stories sometimes serve to protect us from uncomfortable truths, like the way nostalgia for the first Thanksgiving tends to charm white folks out of confronting our ancestors' mistreatment of indigenous people. Or they can offer dignity and hope to the suffering the way recounting Israel's deliverance from Egypt has comforted the Jews through exiles and diasporas and African Americans through slavery and the civil rights movement. Good therapists encourage clients to engage their "storied selves," as research shows people who can construct the events of their lives into redemptive narratives have healthier outcomes. You can pay a consultant several thousand dollars to help your organization determine its "guiding story."

"Whenever humans try to make sense of their experience," wrote Daniel Taylor in his book *Tell Me a Story*, "they create a story, and we use those stories to answer all the big questions of life. The stories come from everywhere—from family, church, school, and the culture at large. They so surround and inhabit us that we often don't recognize that they are stories at all, breathing them in and out as a fish breathes water."[3]

"Every people has a story to tell," wrote theologian James Cone in *God of the Oppressed*, "something to say to themselves, their children, and to the world about how they think and live, as they determine and affirm their reason for being. The story both expresses and participates in the miracle of moving from nothing to something, from nonbeing to being."[4]

Origin stories tell us who we are, where we come from, and what the world is like. They dictate the things we believe, the brands we buy, the holidays we celebrate, and the people we revere or despise. Sometimes we construct our present realities around our stories of origin; other times we construct our stories of origin around our present realities; most of the time it's a little of both. How I understand myself as an American, a Christian, a woman, a mother, a daughter, an introvert, a southerner, a Held, an Evans, and an Alabama Crimson Tide football fan depends largely on the stories I've heard and inherited, and the stories I've told myself. Spiritual maturation requires untangling these stories, sorting fact from fiction (or, more precisely, truth from untruth), and embracing those stories that move us toward wholeness while rejecting or reinterpreting those that do harm.

Activist and theologian Monica Coleman engaged in this untangling in her stunning memoir, *Bipolar Faith*. The memoir begins by locating Coleman's own story of trauma and depression within the context of her family's story, particularly the story of her great-grandfather, a sharecropper from South Carolina who, after the death of his wife, hanged himself in a shed. No one from the family ever took down the noose, so it remained swinging from the rafters for thirty years.

"When I think of growing up in that setting," Coleman wrote of her orphaned grandmother, great-aunts, and great-uncles, "I begin to understand. Every time they played in the shed, they saw the rope. Ten times a day. At least once a week. They got used to it; it became normal—part of their days. And a heaviness hung over each life, and the sadness remained. Like a heavy fog."[5]

No one diagnosed Coleman's great-grandfather with depression—"Who can stop to think of a clinical illness when the children need to be fed?"—but to come to terms with her same diagnosis, Coleman had to reckon with the shadow of that noose and how it taught her early on that "sadness can own you. You can die of grief."[6]

For Coleman, liberation is a tenuous dance, aided by faith, medication, therapy, and supportive relationships. "Now I dance for my own ancestors," she wrote. "I dance for Grandma and Great-Grandaddy. I dance for my great-aunts and great-uncles who lived with the noose. . . . I will dance their tears and their ability to live through them. . . . I will dance the legacy they left me, and the freedom I can eke out."[7]

Coleman's story reminds us there are demons in our stories that can only be cast out when we call them by name.

Indeed, my own Appalachian heritage isn't all folksy bluegrass ballads accompanied by clawhammer banjos. That cold mountain creek crawled through plenty of mobile home parks strewn with broken toys and beer cans, and the blight of alcoholism felled some of my dearest cousins. It was in this community of aunts, uncles, cousins, and great-grandparents that I first heard the N-word muttered with disdain. It's important to identify and unpack these stories—the good and the bad, the true and the half-true—for they explain so much of what we believe and how we behave.

When faced with the decision to hold on to that empty coffee canister or toss it out, my husband, Dan, can recall with gusto a litany of tales from relatives who survived the Great Depression and war rationing to give every item they owned a second or third life. Just yesterday, while lamenting a friendship that had fallen by the wayside, I told myself a story about how I "chose a career over having friends." What an elaborate little tale I'd spun to explain a forgotten birthday! We're all creative writers, you see, dabbling with a bit of fiction here and a bit of nonfiction there to try and make some sense of our lives.

"We tell ourselves stories in order to live," Joan Didion famously wrote. "We look for the sermon in the suicide, for the social or moral lesson in the murder of five. We interpret what we see, select the most workable of the multiple choices. We live entirely, especially if we are writers, by the imposition of a narrative line upon disparate images, by the 'ideas' with which we have learned to freeze the shifting phantasmagoria which is our actual experience."[8]

When we understand the function of origin stories, both in our culture and in our lives, we can make better sense of those found in Scripture. The creation account of Genesis 1, in which God brings order to the cosmos and makes it a temple, is meant to remind the people of Israel, and by extension, us, that God needs no building of stone from which to reign, but dwells in every landscape and in the presence of the humble will make a home. Should all other identities or securities be thrown into tumult, should nations be fractured and temples torn down, this truth remains—God is with us and God is for us. It's a story as true now as it was then.

Of course, we miss all this when we insist the Bible's origin stories are simply straightforward recitations of historical fact, one scientific discovery or archaeological dig away from ruin. What both hardened fundamentalists and strident atheists seem to have in common is the conviction that any trace of myth, embellishment, or cultural influence in an origin story renders it untrue. But this represents a massive misunderstanding of the genre itself.

It's a bit like this: Imagine if, for your birthday, your entire family gathered—parents and siblings, aunts and uncles, cousins and friends—and in celebration of the anniversary of your birth, presented you with a formal reading of your birth certificate.

May 1, 1984. 10:05 a.m. 6 lbs, 14 ounces. Tupelo, Mississippi.

That's it. No dinner. No homemade cards. No cake and ice cream. No long, candle-lit evening retelling those familiar, exaggerated stories about how your dad nearly wrecked the car on the way to the hospital, or how you pooped all over that fancy take-home dress your grandmother made, or how your uncle kept flirting with the nursing staff. No laughter-filled debates over which you said first, "Mama" or "Dada." No internet searches for where the Olympics were held that year and who ran for president. No reminders that you were named after a beautiful shepherdess from the Bible and a stubborn schoolteacher from Appalachia.

Just the facts.

That would be weird, right?

We know who we are, not from the birth certificates and Social Security numbers assigned to us by the government, but from the stories told and retold to us by our community. Should the time of birth on your certificate be off by a minute, or should it be lost altogether, it wouldn't change what's truest about you—that you matter and are loved.

Literary scholar Barbara Hardy said as long ago as 1968, "We dream in narrative, day-dream in narrative, remember, anticipate, hope, despair, believe, doubt, plan, revise, criticize, construct, gossip, learn, hate and love by narrative."[9]

We meet God in narrative too.

The origin stories of Scripture remind us we belong to a very large and very old family that has been walking with God from the beginning. Even when we falter and fall, this God is in it for the long haul. We will not be abandoned.

ᘐ

When I was in second or third grade, the Bible college that employed my father moved locations, converting a recently vacated church building in Birmingham into a campus of offices, dorm rooms, and classrooms. In the moving process, my dad scored all kinds of secondhand finds from those old Sunday school rooms—books, art supplies, boxes of expensive wooden building blocks—treasures he brought home to two adoring little girls every afternoon after work. One day he walked through the door with one of those giant flannelgraph boards used for telling Bible stories. Mounted on a wooden easel, the flannel-covered board could be affixed with sandpaper-backed paper cutouts of biblical characters from the Old and New Testaments, characters like Noah, Abraham, Rachel, Ruth, Jesus, Mary, and Joseph, the colors of their robes faded from years in storage.

My little sister, Amanda, and I spent many barefoot hours in our living room with that board and those cutouts, together reenacting the tales of Abraham's family and Jesus' miracles, often filling in the narratives with our own imaginative stories. (I remember I created a rather dramatic and detailed backstory for the little boy whose lunch of fish and loaves Jesus turned into a meal to feed five thousand, complete with an argument with his mother that morning, an attempted runaway, and a moment of repentance and redemption as he volunteered his lunch for the sake of the gospel.) We invented conversations between Abraham and Isaac as they descended Mount Moriah. We embellished the details of Ruth's courtship with Boaz. We imagined what happened to Zacchaeus after the "wee little man" from our Sunday school song climbed out of his sycamore to follow Jesus.

Little did we know that we were participating in a long tradition of creative engagement with the biblical text, one dating back thousands of years.

Christians can learn a lot about Scripture from the people who have had it the longest. I came to this realization a few years ago when a writing project around the women of the Bible introduced me to *midrash*—those imaginative explorations and expansions of Scripture that serve as the most common form of biblical interpretation in Jewish traditions. These writings, some ancient and some modern, alerted me to details in the text I'd never noticed before, and offered both playful and instructive interpretations of those details that animated the biblical characters in fresh new ways.

For example, the Bible's reference to Leah's "weak eyes" is explained in some midrashic traditions as a sign that Leah's eyes were weak from weeping, for she feared she would be forced to marry the wild scoundrel Esau. The two bracelets Isaac gave to his bride-to-be, Rebekah, are imagined to represent the two tablets upon which the Ten Commandments would be chiseled, a sign of the momentous nature of this union, which would bring the people of the Torah into the world. Abraham is given a colorful backstory by the rabbis who composed midrash, including a famous tale in which, as a boy, he smashed the idols in his father's shop, told his father the mess had been created by the idols fighting one another, and then cleverly exposed the emptiness of idolatry when his father insisted inanimate objects could not war with one another. Even the donkey that accompanied Abraham and Isaac on their fateful trip to Mount Moriah gets a detailed pedigree in one midrash, which suggests the ass descended from the donkey created on the sixth day of creation and is the same animal that spoke to the prophet Balaam, carried Moses as he descended into Egypt, and will one day be mounted by King David when he returns in triumph during the messianic age. That's a busy donkey.

Wilda Gafney, an Episcopal priest and biblical scholar whose book *Womanist Midrash* offers a midrashic interpretation of biblical women rooted in the African American preaching tradition, explained, "Midrash interprets not only the text before the reader, but also the text behind and beyond the text and the text between the lines of the text. In rabbinic thinking, each letter and the spaces between the letters are available for interpretive work."[10]

Midrash, which initially struck me as something of a cross between biblical commentary and fan fiction, introduced me to a whole new posture toward Scripture, a sort of delighted reverence for the text unencumbered by the expectation that it must behave itself to be true. For Jewish readers, the tensions and questions produced by Scripture aren't obstacles to be avoided, but rather opportunities for engagement, invitations to join in the Great Conversation between God and God's people that has been going on for centuries and to which everyone is invited.

I suspect I resonate with midrashic interpretation because it helps me recover some of the curiosity and wonder with which I approached the Bible as a child. It gives me permission to "play" a little with the stories. It also gives me permission to indulge my questions and confront my doubts. For example, it wasn't until I encountered the volumes of midrash around the story of the binding of Isaac that I realized I wasn't alone in my misgivings about that tale in which God tests Abraham by instructing him to sacrifice his only son on an altar, only to send an angel to stay his hand just before Abraham plunges the knife into his son's chest. Readers ancient and modern have struggled with that story, positing different possibilities for why God would ask Abraham to do such a thing. *Was God using Abraham to make a point against the practice of child sacrifice, common among the pagans? Or did Abraham only imagine he heard the voice of God? Was God disciplining Abraham for his treatment of Ishmael? Would Abraham himself have finally relented, before actually committing the act, and would disobedience have ultimately been the right and ethical thing for him to choose? How should parents understand the moral of this unsettling tale?*

As it turns out, Jews believe these questions are up for debate, instructive not only when we arrive at an answer, but when the ensuing discussion reveals something important to us about our faith, our community, and ourselves. While Christians tend to turn to Scripture to *end* a conversation, Jews turn to Scripture to *start* a conversation.

A Jewish friend of mine told of a dinner party in which her husband, a rabbi, invited a group of fellow rabbis, scholars, and friends over for conversation.

"We were debating application of Torah long into the night," she told me. "Everyone brought a different point of view, no one could exactly agree, shouts of hearty agreement and fierce dissent woke the baby twice, and we nearly ran out of food.

"For a group of Jews," she said with a laugh, "it was the perfect evening."

Her story reveals how the biblical text comes alive in the context of community, its endless shades and contours revealed in the presence of a diversity of readers—young and old, learned and unlearned, rich and poor, historic and contemporary, living and dead. This style of engagement not only brings us closer to Scripture's many truths, but closer to one another. The sacred text becomes a crucial point of contact, a great dining room table, erected by God and set by God's people, where those who hunger for nourishment and companionship can gather together and be filled.

"The Bible creates community," wrote Timothy Beal in *The Rise and Fall of the Bible*, "by providing space for community to happen. It offers storied worlds and theological vocabularies around which people can come together in conversation about abiding questions. It calls for creative, collaborative participation."[11]

This attitude stands in stark contrast to the winner-take-all posture in many fundamentalist Christian communities, which positions the solitary reader as objective arbiter of truth, his "straight-forward" reading of the text final and exclusive. The refrain goes something like, "The Bible said it; I believe it; that settles it," which is not exactly the sort of conversation starter that brings people together.

Midrash, with its imaginative engagement of the Bible's stories, reminds us that biblical interpretation need not be reduced to a zero-sum game, but rather inspires endless insights and challenges, the way a good story does each time it is told and retold. Our relational God has given us a relational sacred text, one that, should we surrender to it, reminds us that being people of faith isn't as much about being right as it is about being part of a community in restored and restorative relationship with God. This is how Paul engaged Scripture, after all, and Jesus—both of whom were Jews.

The narrative tradition of Jewish interpretation is supported by the colorful cast of characters that comprises Israel's family of origin, characters whose antics, in the words of Rabbi Visotzky, unfold in the book of Genesis like "the longest-running family soap opera in history."[12] Aunt Ethel and Uncle Wick have nothing on Father Abraham and Mother Sarah—and the children, grandchildren, in-laws, and enemies who populate some of Scripture's most memorable scenes.

As the story goes, God makes a covenant with Abraham, promising to bless him with enough descendants to make a great nation, one whose population would grow to outnumber the stars and would bless every other nation on earth. But Abraham and his wife Sarah are childless and elderly, and rather than trusting God with their fertility, they give Abraham an Egyptian slave named Hagar to impregnate, the result of which is Ishmael, a boy who would grow to be "a wild donkey of a man" (Genesis 16:12). As tensions between Hagar and Sarah escalate, God renews his promise to Abraham to give him a son with Sarah, urging him to remain blameless and upright and to signal his commitment by circumcising his children and their descendants. Sure enough, after many years of waiting, Sarah gives birth to Isaac, who is promptly circumcised.

Sarah dies. Isaac grows up. Abraham arranges for his son to get a good wife, a woman named Rebekah. Isaac and Rebekah give birth to twins—Jacob and Esau—whose epic rivalry begins at delivery, as the younger, smooth-skinned Jacob grasps the heel of the older, hairy Esau on the way out of the birth canal. It's a bit baffling that God would favor Jacob, a quiet and conniving mama's boy who tricks his older brother out of his inheritance rights and deceives his aging father into compliance, but Hebrew Scripture has a soft spot for scrappy underdogs, so he grows into the unlikely hero of Israel's origin stories.

After provoking Esau's rage, Jacob flees to his uncle Laban's home in Paddan Aram, where Jacob falls in love with Laban's beautiful daughter, Rachel, who herself has a complicated relationship with her own sibling, Leah. Laban promises to give Jacob Rachel's hand, but only after he works for his uncle, breeding and tending sheep for seven years, because apparently Jacob is something of an ancient Mesopotamian sheep-whisperer. The wedding day arrives, and of course there is much dancing and drinking and merrymaking, but when Jacob wakes up the next morning to kiss his new bride, "behold, it [is] Leah!" (Genesis 29:25 NASB). The con artist has become the mark. Laban eventually gives Jacob Rachel in exchange for seven more years of work, and predictably, an intense rivalry brews between the sisters. With the help of a couple of handmaids, they give Jacob twelve sons and a daughter. Meanwhile, Esau builds an army.

When twenty years of Laban's hijinks become too much, Jacob decides that an angry brother with an army is better than an opportunistic father-in-law with a bunch of sheep, so he gathers his enormous family, with all their livestock and belongings, and leads them to the desert to return to Canaan.

In this wilderness, between one bad situation and another, Jacob encounters a mysterious stranger.

While camping alone on the river Jabbok, Jacob is roused by what appears to be a man—and a strong one at that—intent on a fight. The two wrestle all through the night, each one gaining the upper hand at one moment only to lose it the next. As dawn breaks and it becomes clear this stranger is no mere "man" but rather the very presence of God, Jacob musters the gall to demand a blessing from his opponent. God relents and delivers a blessing to Jacob in the form of a name change. From now on, Jacob will be known as Israel, which means "He struggles with God." The fighting ends, but not before Jacob sustains an injury to his hip, one that leaves him walking with a limp for the rest of his life. Jacob goes on to make peace with his brother. His twelve sons become the twelve tribes of Israel, and the rest, as they say, is history.

The significance of this story of family origins to the people of Israel cannot be overstated, for it demonstrates how the dynamic, personal, back-and-forth relationship between God and God's people is embedded in their very identity, their very *name—Israel*, "because you have struggled with God and with humans and have overcome" (Genesis 32:28).

"Israel's self-understanding is one of being in a locked battle with God," wrote Peter Enns and Jared Byas in *Genesis for Normal People*. "This is not a people who see themselves as triumphant tops on the food chain, but as a wandering, wondering people who—to use the vernacular of our day—struggle with their faith."[13]

This understanding of themselves as a people who wrestle with God and emerge from that wrestling with both a limp and a blessing informs how Jews engage with Scripture, and it ought to inform how Christians engage Scripture too, for we share a common family of origin, the same spiritual DNA. The biblical scholars I love to read don't go to the holy text looking for ammunition with which to win an argument or trite truisms with which to escape the day's sorrows; they go looking for a blessing, a better way of engaging life and the world, and they don't expect to escape that search unscathed.

"Perhaps we need the angel to start grappling with us," wrote Madeleine L'Engle in *A Stone for a Pillow*, "to turn us aside from the questions which have easy answers to those which cause us to grow, no matter how painful that growth can be."[14]

If I've learned anything from thirty-five years of doubt and belief, it's that faith is not passive intellectual assent to a set of propositions. It's a rough-and-tumble, no-holds-barred, all-night-long struggle, and sometimes you have to demand your blessing rather than wait around for it.

The same is true for Scripture. With Scripture, we've not been invited to an academic fraternity; we've been invited to a wrestling match. We've been invited to a dynamic, centuries-long conversation with God and God's people that has been unfolding since creation, one story at a time. If we're lucky, it will leave us with a limp.

THE WELL

Most of the time, God does the naming.

Abraham. Isaac. Israel.

Just one person in all your sacred Scripture dared to name God, and it wasn't a priest, prophet, warrior, or king. It was I, Hagar—foreigner, woman, slave.[1]

I do not wish to be remembered as powerless, for power is the currency of men; but before the wilderness, before the naming, my station ranked me among the invisible. Dark skin and foreign tongue curried little favor in Beersheba, land of the Seven Wells, where warring tribes marked moments of peace by digging together for water.

I belonged to a woman blessed with all the things a woman wants—wealth, nobility, legendary beauty, and divine favor—but not the thing a woman in an unsettled territory needs: a womb that can carry a boy. Sarah wore her laugh lines like jewelry. She told stories better than anyone I've ever known. The desert wind sent her white hair dancing and carried her unmistakable peals of laughter through the arid atmosphere like rain. Old and young, men and women, slave and free ventured to her tent for advice on breeding goats, arranging marriages, spicing food, and offering prayers. And yet, in our world, they called this woman *barren*.

I had the misfortune to belong to a woman who believed the wrong name.

So she gave my body to Abraham. Long as I live I will never forget how casually she informed me of my duty, rattled off at the end of a list of linens to gather and food to prepare. You will think me callous for not being more angry, more resistant to the charge before me, but bearing the child of a tribal leader, even in another woman's name, carried with it the possibility of more freedom, or at least a challenge to my expendability. The moment the old man rolled away from me—he never once looked me in the eye—I begged the gods of Egypt for a boy. If I survived the birth, I might even live to see him marry. Oh, I begged to every god in every language I knew.

A baby's movements don't begin as kicks, but as subtle, enigmatic flutters; they don't tell you that. So I doubted right until the morning when, lying on my side after another night of fitful dreams, I placed my hands on my belly and felt the sudden, certain impression of a heel. No woman can prepare for the awe of it, the overwhelming surge of joy and fear. Instinctively, I looked around for someone to tell, but of course, no one was there. Then came a second nudge, this one longer and firmer, as if to say, *"Don't you dare think yourself alone, Mama; we're here in this world together."* My baby had yet to take a breath of air, and already we shared a secret. That must have been the moment I started singing, little fractures of the lullabies I remembered from my mother—a woman whose skin, I think, smelled of saffron, and whose voice, I think, was soft and deep as a dove's. (The memories of slaves are dappled ones.)

Perhaps I sang a bit too loudly. Perhaps I carried myself with more confidence than before. Your scribes will say I grew contemptuous of my mistress, but your scribes never asked for my view of it.

The only thing I know is that for every day my belly grew rounder, Sarah's spirit grew stormier, a wind-assailed reed about to break. A slave expects harsh words and withheld rations, but the physical abuse surprised me. Taunts turned to slaps, barked orders to mule whips to the back. I would not have fled had she not threatened the baby's life; I want you to know that. I would not have taken the risk of running into the desert in the dead of night with only a jug of water and some stolen bread to sustain me had I not feared the worst. Abraham did nothing, of course; my mute idols even less. *Did they even notice? Could they even see?*

Your scribes will remember it as a silly women's spat, an anecdote to explain how this cursed land grew populated, but your scribes never carried a baby through the desert. Your scribes never knew the singular desperation of counting the hours from the last assuring kick.

I took the road to Shur, the closest thing I knew to home. But as the sun rose like a great unseeing eye over the fifth or sixth mile, and the weight on my pelvis numbed my legs, I collapsed into the dust.

Water gone, food regurgitated, blood streaking down my thighs, I waited there to die . . . or to deliver . . . or both. *Who will find my body?* I wondered. *And what story will they tell of it?*

Then, on the rippling horizon: a well!

I crawled to it, plunged my face in. I think I must have fainted there, or slept.

All I know is when I opened my eyes, a stranger stood beside me—a presence neither male nor female, neither Egyptian nor Hebrew, neither safe nor threatening—and in a voice that sounded like my mother's, spoke:

"Hagar, slave of Sarah, where have you come from and where are you going?"

This stranger knew my name.

"I am fleeing from my mistress," I answered. What could I say of where I was going?

"Go back to Sarah," the stranger said. "But do not be afraid. Not only will this child live, but through him I will give you a whole nation of descendants, grandchildren and great-grandchildren, too numerous to count."

I cannot tell you why, but immediately I believed. This stranger with the voice of a dove spoke with the authority of God.

"Your son will grow into a fighter," God said, "a wild donkey of a man. But even as he struggles, he will survive. Call him Ishmael, for it means 'God hears,' and God has heard you in your misery today."

In spite of everything, I smiled at the part about the donkey, for already I knew how that boy kicked. Every mama is something of a prophet.

You may think a prophecy of struggle and strife would dishearten a pregnant mother, but a slave does not struggle or strive; a slave only obeys. If the prophecy was true, it meant this boy, my Ishmael, would be free.

With what force I could muster, I rose to face God, the brightness of the sun obscuring both our faces. I knew it was the God of my mistress, whom she called Yahweh, but if I was to be the mother of a nation, I would need to give this God a new name.

"You are a God who not only hears, but also sees," I said, surprised by the strength in my voice. "I have seen the One who sees me."

So I named God as I named the well: El Roi, the God Who Sees.

And it was a name remembered, for as your Scripture reports, "That is why the well was called Beer Lahai Roi. It is still there, between Kadesh and Bered."

Many of my sisters would draw from that well: the Hebrew

midwives who defied Pharaoh by delivering the babies of slaves, the despised Samaritan who scandalized a town for daring to speak to the Messiah, the young women ripped from their homes in West Africa and shipped like livestock across the sea, the mamas who saw their boys lynched and the grandmas who saw their grandsons gunned down, the millions of black and brown people whose names the world has forgotten but whose God never failed to see, the fierce female prophets and preachers who rose from the ashes of their suffering and dared, like me, to survive and to name. I, too, would return to it, years later when Sarah banished me to the wilderness again, this time with a little boy clinging to my legs.

My faith, like Abraham's, was tested. But my faith, unlike the patriarchs, was not immortalized in Caravaggio's reds or Chagall's blues for later generations to view, nor was it remembered in the litany of Hebrews or in the genealogies of your New Testament.

Yet just one person in all your sacred Scripture dared to name God, and it wasn't a priest, prophet, warrior, or king. It was I, Hagar—foreigner, woman, slave.

Don't you dare forget.

2

DELIVERANCE STORIES

W hy is this night different from all other nights?"
The question is traditionally posed by a child, her little
face lit by the candles that adorn the seder table, where family and
friends have gathered to celebrate the Jewish holiday of Passover.

She has watched with curiosity as wine has been poured, prayers
have been prayed, and the matzah—a crackerlike flatbread made
from unleavened flour—has been ceremonially broken into pieces.
The scent of roasted chicken and baked potato casserole wafts
through the house, but the little girl's seder plate remains largely
untouched, its contents including a boiled egg, a shank bone, a
clump of romaine lettuce, a stalk of celery, and a generous helping
of charoset—a mixture of chopped apples, sliced almonds, honey,
and cinnamon that her mother insists she would like if she just gave
it a try.

Everything on the plate represents something. Indeed, everything on the table has a story. The charoset represents the mortar
used by the Hebrew slaves to build Egyptian storehouses, the bowls

of salt water into which the celery is dipped, their tears. Everyone at the table makes a point of leaning back into their chairs, for in ancient times, only wealthy, free men enjoyed the luxury of reclining at the dinner table. Reclining at the seder reminds the Jews that when God delivered their people from slavery, God not only granted them freedom, God made them nobles.

These traditions have provided glimpses of the story, but now that the roast is nearly finished, it is time for the main event, the telling of the story of the exodus from Egypt.

This is the moment the little girl has been waiting for, the moment she is charged with asking, "Why?"

"Why is tonight different from all other nights? Why do we break the matzah and eat the charoset? Why do we recline at the table and sing hymns?"

Her grandfather, or perhaps a grandmother or aunt or a rabbi from synagogue, will straighten up and begin:

"Remember how God promised Abraham that his descendants would outnumber the stars, little one?

"Well, God kept that promise, and sure enough, the people of Israel became a great nation. But after many years, that nation fell into slavery in Egypt, forced into labor by a powerful pharaoh. So God summoned a man named Moses to demand that Pharaoh let the people of Israel go. But Pharaoh was stubborn and cruel. Even after God cursed the Egyptians with plagues of locusts and darkness and pestilence and frogs, even after God turned the Great Nile into a river of blood, Pharaoh would not relent. Finally, God sent an angel of death to visit every home in Egypt, save the homes of the people of Israel, which had been marked with a special sign. Only then did Pharaoh release the slaves, and even then, the people

of Israel had to leave Egypt in such a hurry, they didn't have time to wait for their bread to rise in their ovens, which is why, to this day, Jews eat matzah to remember that first Passover night."

The little girl will hear of how Pharaoh then reneged on his promise and pursued the fleeing people with an army of chariots, how Moses lifted up his staff as God parted the Red Sea, how the forces of Egypt drowned and the people of God escaped, and how the God who was faithful to the people of Israel then will be faithful to them forever.

An uncle or aunt may test the little girl to see if she was listening, but most at the table are ready to move on to the main course and the next glass of wine. The typical seder will last long into the night. It is said that even in the concentration camps of Poland during World War II, Passover was observed. Even there, without food or wine or candlelight, the Jews reclined.

The story of the exodus, of the escape of the Israelites from the grip of Pharaoh, is perhaps the best known of the Bible's deliverance stories. The tale has long been central to Jewish identity and ethic, recounted daily in prayers and annually with the celebration of Passover. Throughout the Bible, God self-identifies with the people of Israel as "the LORD your God, who brought you out of Egypt, out of the land of slavery" (Deuteronomy 5:6). This single event, whether historical or legendary or a bit of both, has shaped the faith of millions of people, inspiring artists and activists and world leaders for centuries. Never should it be discounted as *just* a story.

Indeed, these ancient words of liberation—"Let my people go"—first uttered by premodern people in an unforgiving desert eons ago, traveled over time and space to reach the ears and lips of another enslaved population, laboring in the cotton fields of Alabama, who sang and then shouted back:

> *Go down, Moses,*
> *Way down to Egypt's land,*
> *Tell old Pharaoh,*
> *Let my people go.*

Few of the enslaved African Americans who first sang this and other Christian spirituals knew the full biblical context from which they emerged. American slave owners had a vested interest in keeping their "property" illiterate, and even free blacks, like Frederick Douglass and Henry Highland Garnet, debated the wisdom of distributing Scripture among the people whose bondage was often justified with citations of Ephesians 6:5—"Slaves, obey your earthly masters with respect and fear . . . just as you would obey Christ."

As Allen Dwight Callahan explained in his masterful work *The Talking Book: African Americans and the Bible,* "African Americans found the Bible to be both healing balm and poison book. They could not lay claim to the balm without braving the poison. . . . The antidote to hostile texts of the Bible was more Bible, homeopathically administered to counteract the toxins of the text."[1]

The story of the exodus inspired some of the most effective rhetoric of the abolition movement in the nineteenth century and the civil rights movement in the twentieth century, with Moses' call to "let my people go" echoing with new force from the lips of Harriet Tubman, Frederick Douglass, James Weldon Johnson, and Martin Luther King Jr. In addition, biblical figures like Joseph, who triumphed over slavery, and Daniel, delivered from Nebuchadnezzar's lions' den, figure prominently in black music, literature, and preaching, and a single line from Psalm 68—"Ethiopia shall soon stretch out her hands unto God"—came to signify God's promise of a glorious future for people of African descent (v. 31 KJV). Generations of Christian African Americans have found solidarity and empowerment in the death and resurrection of Jesus Christ, with liberationist theologian James Cone making a striking connection between the crucifixion of Jesus and the scourge of lynching against black men. And, as womanist theologian Delores Williams elucidated in her landmark book, *Sisters in the Wilderness,* the character of Hagar—an African slave who was brutalized by her masters and forced into surrogacy—serves as a symbolic counterpart to the perilous experiences of many African American women, past and present.

Allen Dwight Callahan observed,

> African slaves and their descendants discerned something in the Bible that was neither at the center of their ancestral cultures nor in evidence in their hostile American home, a warrant for justice in this world. They found woven in the texts of the Bible a crimson thread of divine justice antithetical to the injustice they had come to know all too well.[2]

This crimson thread of justice has been traced by marginalized people through the ages, their struggle for freedom sustained by Scripture's call to honor the poor, welcome the stranger, and liberate the oppressed. For centuries the Bible's stories of deliverance have offered hope to the struggling—from enslaved African Americans who saw the promise of freedom in the story of the exodus, to pioneering women in ministry who found affirmation in Mary Magdalene's role as apostle to the apostles, to poor, rural Latin American farmers who resonated with Christ's declaration that he came to proclaim "good news to the poor . . . to set the oppressed free" and developed a theology of liberation around that theme (Luke 4:18). My Jewish friends like to joke that you can sum up nearly every Jewish holiday with, "They tried to kill us; we won; let's eat!" If you've ever celebrated a Passover seder or watched a raucous reenactment of the story of Esther at the Purim festival, you know that God's preference for the underdog, for defending the defenseless and championing the cause of the suffering, is a biblical theme too common to ignore.

The rich history of reading new meaning into the Bible's deliverance stories reminds us, too, that in an effort to understand the unique context from which Scripture emerged and the original audience for whom it was intended, we dare not forgo the long and crucial tradition of sacred appropriation, of allowing these ancient stories to speak fresh life into new, fitting, contexts. After all, Scripture is described as the *living* Word of God (Hebrews 4:12), which means it remains animated and active, pulsing with possibility. In the same way the lines from great literature have a way of transcending their original context to cast light into the contours of a new one ("These violent delights have violent ends," "And so we beat on, boats against the current," "What happens to a dream deferred?"), the words of Scripture have been recalibrated and remixed through the centuries to comfort, challenge, and enlighten all kinds of communities of faith.

In other words, Bible stories don't have to mean just one thing. Despite what you may have heard from a pastor or Sunday school teacher along the way, faithful engagement with Scripture isn't about uncovering a singular, moralistic point to every text and then sticking to it. Rather, the very nature of the biblical text invites us to consider the possibilities.

"Turn it and turn it," the ancient rabbis said of Scripture, comparing it to a precious gem, "for everything is in it."[3]

Of course, the fact that a single biblical text can mean many things doesn't mean it can mean *anything*. Slave traders justified the exploitation of black people by claiming the curse on Noah's son Ham rendered all Africans subhuman. Many Puritans and pioneers appealed to the stories of Joshua's conquest of Canaan to support attacks on indigenous populations. More recently, I've heard Christians shrug off sins committed by American politicians because King David assaulted women too. Anytime the Bible is used to justify the oppression and exploitation of others, we have strayed far from the God who brought the people of Israel out of Egypt, "out of the land of slavery" (Exodus 20:2).

This is why it's especially important for those of us who come to the Bible from positions of relative social, economic, and racial privilege to read its stories alongside people from marginalized communities, past and present, who are often more practiced at tracing that crimson thread of justice through its pages.

"I do theology as a matter of survival," explained Rev. Broderick Greer, who is black and gay, "because if people can do theology that produces brutality against black, transgender, queer, and other minority bodies, then we can do theology that leads to our common liberation."[4]

I confess that until recently I didn't see it this way. I grew up in a world where every pastor I knew was white and male, every theologian I admired came from Western cultures, every Bible study I attended was held in sprawling suburban homes. Rarely did I hear the words of Scripture spoken in an accent other than my own, and when it came time to color the faces of Moses, Mary, and Jesus in my coloring books, I reached for "peach." As a result, I failed to see important patterns of oppression and liberation not only in the Bible, but also in the world around me. I remained complicit in systems of injustice that hurt my neighbors of color, and those with disabilities, and those living in the developing world because I hadn't learned to center their stories, to see things from their point of view.

Social media gets a bad rap, often deservedly so, but when you're a white, twentysomething southerner who lives in the same town where she attended high school and thinks Coldplay is "lit," it can also expand your horizons. Online I encountered writers, activists, pastors, and biblical scholars who masterfully appealed to Scripture to advocate for social justice and reconciliation, and who prioritized in their work and imaginations biblical characters I'd never really noticed before—characters like the daughters of Zelophehad, who successfully lobbied the leaders of Israel for the right for women to inherit property, and the Ethiopian eunuch from the book of Acts, whose status as an ethnic and sexual minority makes his dramatic baptism especially meaningful to those who have been treated as outsiders. I had never before considered that Joseph, the despised brother with the coat of many colors, was a victim of human trafficking, or that Jesus himself was once, as a child, a refugee.

Articles online led me to books, which led me to conferences, which led me to dinner table conversations and worship services and protests. Not all of these experiences have been comfortable, of course. Often a speaker or writer will say something that jars me. I'm still learning, still getting things wrong. But sometimes God knows the kind of deliverance you need the most is deliverance from your own comfort.

In her memoir, *Still*, Lauren Winner described a time when she attended a protest on Holy Thursday outside an immigration detention center in North Carolina. Someone from the group read 1 Corinthians 13—*"Love is patient, love is kind"*—and suddenly, those familiar words typically reserved for weddings and Valentine's Day cards took on a new, subversive weight. It was a reminder that "when Paul said Love, he was not speaking about a feeling or even a way of treating the people close to you; when Paul said Love, he was speaking about the identity of another man who was once arrested on Holy Thursday."[5]

This method of engaging Scripture in unexpected places she called "dislocated exegesis." She told of reading the gospel's healing narratives in the Duke oncology unit and the story of the Tower of Babel at the Bank of America Corporate Center in Charlotte. Encountering familiar passages in striking environments can "unsettle the assumptions you were likely to bring to the text," she wrote. "Where you read changes how you read."[6]

They say art should afflict the comfortable and comfort the afflicted. I think the same is true for Scripture. For centuries the Bible's stories of deliverance have offered comfort to the suffering and a challenge to the privileged. Every item on the seder plate and every line from those old spirituals is a reminder that Scripture never ceases to speak fresh truth, and that when it comes to seeking our common liberation, there is no such thing as *just* a story.

∿

When God broke open the firmament and unleashed torrents of water to flood the whole earth, Noah and his family took refuge in an ark. It rained for forty days and forty nights before they were delivered.

After Moses liberated the Hebrew slaves and Pharaoh's army drowned in the sea, the freed people complained and disobeyed. They wandered the desert for forty years before God led them to the promised land, and at last they were delivered . . . again.

When the carpenter's son from Nazareth had been baptized, and Galilee buzzed with rumors of a Messiah, Jesus went out into the wilderness, where Satan tempted him with the enticements the

Son of God would face in the course of his mission: security, fame, and power. Like Moses and Elijah, Jesus fasted for forty days and forty nights before he was delivered.

But before the baptism and temptations, before God became flesh and lived among us, an angel told Mary she was pregnant. Mary carried God in her womb for around forty weeks before, as Luke reports, "the days were accomplished that she should be delivered" (2:6 KJV).

The number forty carries special significance in Scripture, particularly in its deliverance stories. Rather than an exact enumeration of time, forty symbolizes a prolonged period of hardship, waiting, and wandering—a liminal space between the start of something and its fruition that often brings God's people into the wilderness, into the wild unknown.

I, too, was called into a forty-week wilderness of sorts, when just a few months after enduring the heartache of a miscarriage, I found myself sitting on the bathroom floor, staring once again at a little pink cross on a pregnancy test, my heart pounding so loud I was sure the neighbors could hear it.

I plugged the numbers into an app on my phone. "Congratulations!" it chirped. "Your baby is the size of a lentil."

Calling to mind the image of a single brown seed, imagining its weightless presence in the palm of my hand, I felt a sudden wave of nausea. Could anything be more fragile, more helpless? How could something so small take up so much space in my mind and heart?

"Way to go!" my phone buzzed four weeks later. "Your baby is the size of a kumquat!"

I had to google kumquat.

And on it went, for forty long weeks—a veritable cornucopia of verdurous approximations meant to congratulate the expectant mother on the advancement of forces largely out of her control.

Avocado.

Turnip.

Spaghetti squash.

Rutabaga.

Eggplant.

I half expected our OB to look over my legs after that last, long push in the delivery room and declare, "Congratulations! It's a canary melon!"

Every parent processes a miscarriage differently, but mine left me with a deep distrust of my own body and, aided by the requisite surge of hormones, a near-paralyzing anxiety throughout my second pregnancy. At night I turned our bedsheets inside out and upside down, tossing through fitful dreams, and during the day, I obsessed over every subtle shift in ligament pain, every excruciating hour between those reassuring in utero hiccups and kicks. It seemed every conceivable story of pregnancy complication or loss found its way to my social media feed, and as my skin stretched over my belly, it was as if it became more porous, more absorbent of the suffering of others, particularly the mothers and children whose flight from violence in Syria and Iraq occupied the news hour each night. I've always had an active imagination, but pregnancy sent it into overdrive, the scenarios it conjured enough to impress the most ambitious horror novelist. By week thirty, I'd committed to memory the "Complications" index in *What to Expect When You're Expecting*, annoyed by the omission of *existential crisis* between *eclampsia* and *fatigue*.

For nine long months, this mix of excitement and fear pulsed through me. I used to tell people my favorite sound was a train whistle echoing off the mountains in the distance, but now it is, unequivocally, the steady throb of a baby's heartbeat from a fetal

Doppler. How I lived to hear that sweet cadence fill the exam room every two weeks!

Our son was born in early February, on Candlemas Day, which for many liturgical Christians marks the conclusion of the nativity seasons of Advent, Christmas, and Epiphany. Lumbering through the third trimester during this auspicious period stoked in me a new affection for Mary of Nazareth and transformed the words of the familiar King James account into a hopeful mantra, a rubbing stone in my pocket:

"And so it was, that, while they were there, the days were accomplished that she should be delivered."

The days were accomplished.

What volumes hid between those lines! The morning sickness, the hormones, the round ligament pain, the sleepless nights, the anxiety, the fear, those first startling kicks and those first piercing cries—all the quotidian challenges of pregnancy, punctuated by the considerable risks of first-century maternity and the momentous prophecy surrounding this particular child.

Did Mary ever doubt what she'd been told by the angel? Did she wake one night to blood too early or to pain too sharp and wonder if her song had been nothing more than the foolish ramblings of misplaced hope?

There are few doctrines of the Christian faith more astounding to me than the incarnation, the remarkable notion that the God of the universe was once vulnerable as a fetus and hungry as a baby. Mary knew the humanity of Christ more intimately than anyone, from the moment that humanity manifested itself in the swelling of her breasts, a sudden sensitivity to heat and smell, that strange aversion to eggs and insatiable craving for lamb.

"The days were accomplished that she should be delivered."

Two millennia later, in the longest hours of my own

unremarkable pregnancy, this little string of words from the gospel of Luke invited me to press on, to fear not. It reminded me that whether it's a forty-year journey through the wilderness or a forty-week gestation, the most important tasks of life are accomplished a day at a time. Deliverance is as much a transformation of the heart as it is a transference of the body.

This tradition of connecting the Bible's stories of deliverance with stories from one's own experience is a long and crucial one, perhaps best captured in that moment when, in many Christian traditions, a preacher looks out on her bustling congregation and asks, "Does anybody have a testimony?"

What follows is a sacred time of call-and-response confession, as the people of God recount their stories of deliverance—from the grip of illness, from the temptation to covet or steal, from addiction, from a bad break, from a cruel employer, from that water bill that without a miracle would never have been paid on time.

"God made a way where there seemed to be no way," it is said. "God saw me through."

These testimonies may seem like small potatoes compared to the testimonies of Moses, Hagar, and Mary, but as counselors and neuroscientists continue to confirm, the ability to shape a narrative from your experiences, and to connect your story to a greater one, is essential for developing empathy, a sense of purpose, and well-being. In fact, some therapists have begun incorporating into their counseling sessions what professor and therapist Makungu M. Akinyela termed "testimony therapy" by encouraging clients to channel the communal, hope-driven spirit of Sunday morning testimony time. Every time we retell stories of God's faithfulness in the past, whether around a candlelit seder table or under a bright, red-and-white-striped revival tent, we are reminded that if God can make a way for Moses and the Hebrew slaves, for Harriet Tubman and the

Underground Railroad, for the grandma living on Social Security, for the alcoholic marking twenty years sober, and for the strung-out pregnant lady mumbling incoherently about rutabagas, then maybe God can make a way for me too. Storytelling always has been, and always will be, one of humanity's greatest tools for survival.

But be warned. In Scripture, and in life, the road to deliverance nearly always takes a detour. Rarely do the people of God reach any kind of promised land without a journey or two through the wilderness.

The wilderness, as both a geographic region and a literary motif, appears in so many of the Bible's stories and poems, it functions a bit like a recurring musical theme—like the swelling strings from *Lawrence of Arabia*. Some biblical characters, like Hagar and Jacob, fled to the wilderness to escape troubled relationships or oppression; others, like the people of Israel, were banished there as part of God's discipline for sin. The prophet Elijah hid in the wilderness to escape political persecution, and Jesus retreated there to fast and pray in preparation for his public ministry. Yes, even God, when clothed with the vulnerability of a human body, spent time in the wild.

In the Bible, the wilderness is a place of danger and desolation, creeping with wild animals and threatening with rugged, parched terrain. In life, it's that long journey through grief, those years between calls with your grown kid, a season of caregiving that stretches your reservoirs of patience and perseverance, the aftermath of the divorce, the season of doubt, the period in between jobs or in between relationships or in between diagnosis and healing. In the wilderness, God can seem very far away, or absent altogether. It may take weeks, months, or even years to get on track again. In the meantime, every well, every drop of manna, every raven bearing bread in its beak, is salvation.

As Walter Brueggemann, renowned theologian and Old

Testament scholar, said, "Like manna, [God's] wilderness presence is always enough on which to survive, but not too much. Like manna, he can be graciously received but not stored or presumed upon. Like manna, it is given out of fidelity but never fully seen and controlled."[7]

The wilderness, by design, *disorients*. As any wilderness trekker past or present will tell you, the wilderness has a way of forcing the point, of bringing to the surface whatever fears, questions, and struggles hide within. Nothing strips you down to your essential humanity and inherent dependency quite like submitting to the elements, surrendering to the wild. In the wilderness, you find out what you are made of and who your friends are. You are forced to leave behind all nonessentials, to quiet yourself and *listen*.

"In our culture of constant access and nonstop media nothing feels more like a curse from God than time in the wilderness," wrote pastor Jonathan Martin in his book *Prototype*. "Our society tells us that if and when we get 'there'—the job or position or degree we've always wanted—that's when all the important stuff will start happening. Not so. All the good stuff happens in obscurity."[8]

Indeed, some of Scripture's most momentous events occur not at the start of a journey, nor at the destination, but in between, in the wilderness. Jacob wrestles with the mysterious stranger. Moses encounters the burning bush. The Israelites receive the Law that will shape them as a people for millennia to come. It is in the wilderness that John the Baptist, complete with locusts in his beard and honey on his lips, baptizes repentant sinners and prepares the world for Jesus, channeling the prophet Isaiah by declaring, "A voice . . . [is] calling in the wilderness. 'Prepare the way of the Lord, make straight paths for him'" (Matthew 3:3).

The people of God would do well to listen to those who have sojourned in the outskirts.

It's worth noting that at the culmination of nearly every wilderness journey is a naming. After receiving a new name of his own, Jacob, now called Israel, names the place where he wrestled with God *Peniel,* which means "face of God." Hagar names the well of her salvation *Beer Lahai Roi,* "I have seen the God who sees me." So when we join with our spiritual ancestors in telling our stories of deliverance, we must remember to name each wilderness, to mark those spots where, when all hope seemed lost, we encountered God—at a desert well on the road to Egypt; on a bridge in Selma, Alabama; at a shabby airport chapel in Chicago; in a labor and delivery room on Candlemas Day.

God makes a way where there seems to be no way.

It's the steady refrain of our narrative heritage.

What verses will your story add to it? What wells will your journey name?

ᕫ

If you were attempting one of those Bible-in-a-year programs where you read through all sixty-six books of the Protestant Bible chronologically, in 365 days, you will at this point have followed the story of Israel from its primordial beginnings, to the establishment of Abraham as the father of a great nation, to the liberation of his descendants from slavery in Egypt, to God's giving of the Ten Commandments at Mount Sinai. You have survived the Great Flood in the shelter of Noah's ark, wandered with Hagar through the unforgiving desert, and endured the endless "begets" of several Old Testament genealogies.

The good news is you've done a lot of reading. The bad news is you've reached the point at which even the most devoted readers usually turn back—the Law.

For me, it's Exodus 21 that always does me in, in particular the detailed restitution laws regarding livestock.

If someone's ox kills another person's ox, the law says, then the two owners are to sell the live ox and divide the earnings, then split the dead ox. But "if it is known that the ox has been accustomed to gore in the past, and its owner has not kept it in, he shall repay ox for ox, and the dead beast shall be his" (Exodus 21:36 ESV).

Seems fair enough.

If an ox gores a man or woman to death, the ox must be stoned and its flesh discarded, but the owner of the ox should not be held liable unless the owner knew he had a problem ox, in which case the owner must also be stoned to death.

Well that's a little harsh.

And if an ox kills a slave, then the ox must be stoned and its owner ordered to compensate the slave owner thirty silver shekels.

So what's streaming on Netflix right now?

Christians have long struggled with exactly how to interpret and receive what is commonly referred to as "the Law" of Hebrew Scripture. Almost a third of the first five books of the Bible consists of these laws, which cover everything from crime to property to sexual behavior to humanitarianism to holidays, and which the early rabbis tallied at 613 commands. The Talmud enumerated the Law thusly: "Six hundred thirteen commandments were revealed to Moses; 365 being prohibitions equal in number to the days of the year, and 248 being mandates corresponding in number to the bones of the human body" (Babylonian Talmud Makkot 23b).

For Jews, "law is the lifeblood of the tradition," wrote Douglas A. Knight in *The Meaning of the Bible*, "the pulse that is continually checked, discussed, interpreted, and compared with other parts of the tradition."[9] Franz Rosenzweig famously taught that, in the Jewish community, there are only two answers to the question, "Do you observe the *mitzvot* (commands of God)?" The first answer is "Yes." The other answer is "Not yet." Of course, within Judaism, a multiplicity of interpretations and applications of the Law exist, ranging from Orthodox traditions that keep it quite strictly, to Reform traditions that value the Law's ethical teachings without enforcing, say, kosher laws that forbid the eating of certain foods. But the overriding consensus is that the Law is God's gift to the Jewish people, given as a sign of God's special, covenant relationship with them.

Christians, on the other hand, have a rockier relationship with Old Testament Law. Conservatives are quick to cite it when condemning same-sex behavior or supporting the display of the Ten Commandments in federal courthouses, while progressives like me tend to shrug it off as outdated and irrelevant until we need a quote about "welcoming the stranger" to scribble on a protest sign. We've all been known to plead, "Christians aren't under the Law!" when skeptics remind us that the Torah condemns wearing mixed fibers and allows for stoning disobedient children, yet most of us have committed to memory the famous Shema Prayer—"You shall love the LORD your God with all your heart and with all your soul and with all your strength" (taken from Deuteronomy 6:5). Many Christians, influenced by the writings of Martin Luther, believe the Law represents all that is wrong with legalistic "religion" and argue that the majority of the content of the first five books of the Bible is useful only for showing that humans are incapable of pleasing God and thus in need of a savior like Jesus.

I'm convinced Christians arrive at these malnourished understandings of biblical Law whenever we remove the Law from its narrative context. The Bible's "thou-shalt-nots" weren't delivered in a vacuum, after all, but from Mount Sinai, in the wilderness between Egypt and the promised land. When God gave the people of Israel the Ten Commandments, God began by reminding them, "I am the LORD your God, who brought you out of Egypt, out of the land of slavery" (Exodus 20:2). The Law is an extension of God's liberation of the Hebrew slaves, the continuation of their deliverance story. As Walter Brueggemann observed, "The commandments of Sinai are always grounded in the surprise of liberation from Egypt. If one does not believe in the surprise of liberation, then the endless multiplications of commandments from Sinai is silly, for more commandments without the foundation of the Exodus story will never create a community of well-being."[10]

We don't tend to think of law as liberating, but for the people of Israel, these divine instructions helped forge a unique national identity, one wholly distinct from the cultures around them, including the Egyptian Empire that for so long oppressed them. It reminded them, too, that the God who parted the Red Sea and conquered Pharaoh's armies was sticking around for the long haul. This is not a God who liberates, then leaves. This is a God who walks with people through the desert in a cloud of smoke and fire and who literally sets up camp with them in the form of a traveling tabernacle. This is a God who cares about every detail of their new life together, right down to the management of their oxen.

Deliverance, it seems, is not a onetime deal.

The law taught the Israelites how to rest on the Sabbath, treat immigrants with compassion, and celebrate their deliverance story through rituals and holidays. It called them to worship one God, denouncing all forms of idolatry, and to honor that God with a community characterized by order and neighborliness. In an ancient world that often celebrated violent indulgence, the Law offered a sense of stability and moral purpose.

For example, the famous *lex talionis*, "an eye for an eye and a tooth for a tooth" (from Leviticus 24:20), may strike modern readers as a barbaric endorsement of revenge, but within its cultural context, this "law of retaliation" represented a deliberate move away from the excessive punishment allowed in other tribes by limiting retaliatory action to judicious, in-kind responses. In other words, *you can demand restitution for your loss, but no more; this is about justice, not revenge.* The law also limited kings' accumulation of wealth, issued special protections for orphans and widows, and required that laborers were paid fairly and promptly. It even proposed a year of Jubilee every fifty years, in which prisoners and slaves would be freed, debts would be forgiven, and wealth would be redistributed. (Whether this proposal was ever honored is a matter of debate.)

Of course, not every law comes with a discernible progressive subtext. Even after the people of Israel had been delivered from slavery, they themselves chose to own slaves. While Hebrew slaves were released after seven years, slaves acquired in wars with other nations were treated as no more than property, with considerably fewer rights. Laws around rape, virginity, marriage, and divorce reflected patriarchal norms that no doubt harmed many thousands of women whose bodies and lives belonged to the men who owned them and could do with them what they pleased. Capital punishment awaited those who committed adultery, acted as false prophets, or rebelled against their parents.

While it is shortsighted to discount Scripture's laws as totally backward and amoral, it is just as misguided to pretend they reflect a more just society than they do. No one who values the inherent worth and dignity of their fellow human beings should want a return to ancient Israel. Those were not the "good old days." Not by a long shot.

Even the Bible's stories of deliverance cast some troubling shadows. Death may have passed over the homes of the enslaved Hebrews, but it ravaged Egyptian families, taking all their firstborn sons without mercy. Many womanist scholars note that Hagar's liberation is incomplete, for she was told by God to return to her cruel masters. And as we shall see in the next chapter, the very people who based their identity on God's liberating work in their lives would turn to xenophobia, violence, and enslavement to conquer new territory and claim it as their own.

The good news is that God's grand story of deliverance—the deliverance of all people from the bondage of sin (by which I mean our individual and collective bondage to violence, power, fear, hate, greed, and so on)—continues, and Christians believe it reached a new climax at the top of another mountain, where a descendent of these same Hebrew slaves declared:

> You have heard that it was said, "Eye for eye, and tooth for tooth."
> But I tell you, do not resist an evil person. If anyone slaps you on
> the right cheek, turn the other cheek also.... You have heard that
> it was said, "Love your neighbor and hate your enemy." But I tell
> you, love your enemies and pray for those who persecute you,
> that you may be children of your Father in heaven. (Matthew
> 5:38–39, 43–45)

Jesus made it clear that he did not come to abolish the laws of the Torah, "but to fulfill them" (Matthew 5:17). The life and teachings of Jesus, then, embody all that these laws were intended to be. Jesus is what the living, breathing will of God looks like. This includes compassion for the poor, esteem for women, healing for the sick, and solidarity with the suffering. It means breaking bread with outcasts and embracing little children. It means choosing forgiveness over retribution, the cross over revenge, and cooking breakfast for the friend who betrayed you. As Elton Trueblood put it, "The historic Christian doctrine of the divinity of Christ does not simply mean that Jesus is like God. It is far more radical than that. It means that God is like Jesus."[11]

When Jesus was challenged by the experts on the Law to give an answer for what Scripture is all about, he offered a very straightforward, very Jewish response. Quoting Deuteronomy 6 and Leviticus 19, he replied, "'Love the Lord your God with all your heart and with all your soul and with all your mind.' This is the first and greatest commandment. And the second is like it: 'Love your neighbor as yourself.' All the Law and the Prophets hang on these two commandments" (Matthew 22:37–40).

This is the point of every liberation, every wandering through the desert, every law about oxen and yeast and blood. To *love* is to honor God and keep God's commandments. *Love* is the law that liberates slave and slaveholder alike. *Love* is the ultimate deliverance story, for only love can sustain the sojourner out of Egypt, through the desert, up the mountain, and into the promised land.

The truth is, you can bend Scripture to say just about anything you want it to say. You can bend it until it breaks. For those who count the Bible as sacred, interpretation is not a matter of *whether* to pick and choose, but *how* to pick and choose. We're all selective. We all wrestle with how to interpret and apply the Bible to our lives. We all go to the text looking for something, and we all have a tendency to find it. So the question we have to ask ourselves is this: are we reading with the prejudice of love, with Christ as our model, or are we reading with the prejudices of judgment and power, self-interest and greed? Are we seeking to enslave or liberate, burden or set free?

If you are looking for Bible verses with which to support slavery, you will find them. If you are looking for verses with which to abolish slavery, you will find them. If you are looking for verses with which to oppress women, you will find them. If you are looking for verses with which to honor and celebrate women, you will find them. If you are looking for reasons to wage war, there are plenty. If you are looking for reasons to promote peace, there are plenty more. If you are looking for an outdated and irrelevant ancient text, that's exactly what you will see. If you are looking for truth, that's exactly what you will find.

This is why there are times when the most instructive question to bring to the text is not, *What does this say?* but, *What am I looking for?* I suspect Jesus knew this when he said, "Ask and it will be given to you; seek and you will find; knock and the door will be opened to you" (Matthew 7:7).

If you want to do violence in this world, you will always find the weapons. If you want to heal, you will always find the balm. With Scripture, we've been entrusted with some of the most powerful stories ever told. How we harness that power, whether for good or evil, oppression or liberation, changes everything.

THE WALLS

What took the walls of Jericho down?

Was it the shouts of a holy army, the guttural drone of seven shofars, the weight of God in the marching of human feet against a mighty empire's fortress? Or a ragtag gang of mercenaries, hungry for plunder, who talked a prostitute into betraying her people and unlocking the door?

It depends on who tells the story.

Who conquered the city of Jerusalem in 1099?

Was it crusaders on a mission from God to claim the Holy Land for Christ? Or unwitting soldiers sent by Rome to grow its coffers, so crazed by hunger, zealotry, and the promise of heaven that they massacred every living thing in their path until the blood of Muslims and Jews flowed through the streets?

It depends on who tells the story.

And who took Jerusalem back eighty years later?

Was it the city's original inhabitants, intent on avenging their grandparents and restoring their caliphate? Or followers of a false religion whose presence desecrates sacred ground to this day?

It depends on who tells the story.

What spirit carried ships to the shores of the New World and carved the American West with railway lines and wagon ruts?

Was it divine providence and pioneering grit? Or an evil, invading force that brought violence, illness, and plunder to the people for whom the land had always been home?

What set fire to Dresden, buried Tora Bora, and sank the Spanish Armada? What stained the fields of Gettysburg with blood?

For every battle a thousand tales could be told, yet we seldom hear more than one of them.

What took the walls of Jericho down?

Only God, who holds every story, knows.

3

WAR STORIES

In the predawn hours of May 26, 1637, an army of English settlers under the leadership of Captain John Mason breached the palisade walls of a Pequot village near the Mystic River, and with the help of native allies, set fire to the community. Hundreds of Pequot burned alive, and those who managed to escape were shot or slain by Mason's men. Recounting his role in the massacre, Puritan John Underhill wrote, "Down fell men, women, and children. . . . Should not Christians have more mercy and compassion? . . . Sometimes the Scripture declareth women and children must perish with their parents. . . . We had sufficient light from the word of God for our proceedings."[1]

For Underhill and other European colonialists, that "sufficient light" came from the Bible's war stories, particularly those of Israel's battles in Canaan.

As the story of Scripture moves from Israel's most ancient origins to its distant history, the theme shifts from deliverance to conquest. After the death of Moses, God commissioned a warrior named

Joshua to assume leadership over the people of Israel and take possession of the land they had been promised, land stretching "from the desert to Lebanon, and from the great river, the Euphrates . . . to the Mediterranean Sea" (Joshua 1:4). The only problem? This land was already occupied. Various indigenous tribes, known collectively as the Canaanites, had dominated the landscape for years, some boasting mighty armies and fortified cities. It was even rumored that giants walked among them. But God told Joshua, "I will give you every place where you set your foot. . . . I will never leave you nor forsake you. Be strong and courageous, because you will lead these people to inherit the land I swore to their ancestors to give them" (Joshua 1:3, 5–6).

So Joshua led the people onward, crossing the River Jordan, then attacking the city of Jericho—not by charging its gates, but by marching around its walls seven times, blowing rams' horns, and shouting as God had instructed. Sure enough, just as the famous song declares, the walls of Jericho came a-tumblin' down. The text reports that Joshua's army "destroyed with the sword every living thing in it—men and women, young and old, cattle, sheep and donkeys" (Joshua 6:21). Only Rahab, a prostitute, and her family were spared because they had sheltered Israelite spies ahead of the siege. (A children's book in my home provides a G-rated version of the story, explaining that Rahab was able to help because she "often had visitors coming and going at odd hours.")

From Jericho, Joshua's armies moved on to Ai, which they conquered in their second attempt, the first having been compromised by a soldier who broke God's commands regarding plunder. After luring the men of Ai out of the city for ambush, a battalion of Israelite soldiers set fire to the city where the women and children had been left behind, reducing it to "a permanent heap of ruins" (Joshua 8:28). According to the story, the Israelites killed all twelve thousand of the city's inhabitants. The Israelites then offered thanks at Mount Ebal before heading south, where they defeated an alliance of Amorite kingdoms and hung the decapitated bodies of enemy kings from trees. The text reports God sent a hailstorm to pummel the Amorite army and froze the sun in the sky for a full twenty-four hours so Israel would be victorious (Joshua 10).

All told, the Israelites took control of more than thirty Canaanite cities. The last major challenge lay in Hazor, where a coalition of Canaanites had united against the Israelite invaders and rallied an army "as numerous as the sand on the seashore" (11:4). But even with the odds against them, the armies of Israel prevailed, totally destroying the city, killing in it "all who breathed" (10:40). Of Israel's conquest of Canaan, the text notes, "Except for the Hivites living in Gibeon, not one city made a treaty of peace with the Israelites, who took them all in battle. For it was the LORD himself who hardened their hearts to wage war against Israel, so that he might destroy them totally, exterminating them without mercy, as the LORD had commanded Moses" (11:19–20).

It's an astounding statement, and if we encountered it anywhere other than the Bible, we would immediately condemn it as a defense of genocide.

When it comes to processing these troubling stories, there are generally three types of people: (1) those who accept without question that God ordered the military campaigns in Canaan and has likely supported others throughout history, (2) those who are so troubled by the notion of God condoning ethnic cleansing that it strains their faith or compels them to abandon it, (3) those who can name all of the Kardashian sisters and are probably happier for it. I fit rather decidedly into the second category, the Bible's tales of violence and holy war adding some of the first wrinkles to my pristinely starched faith.

Growing up, I noticed the ugly details in the Sunday school stories; children always do. I remember I was deeply troubled by the fact that God drowned all but two of each kind of animal in the Great Flood (to say nothing of all the people), and wondered aloud at the dinner table how God could be all-knowing and all-powerful, but also filled with regret. A friend's seven-year-old captured the angst well when she recently asked, "Mom, is God the good guy or the bad guy in this story?"

This question of God's character haunted every scene and every act and every drama of the Bible. It wasn't just the story of Noah's flood or Joshua's conquests that unsettled me. The book of Judges recounts several horrific war stories in which women's bodies are used as weapons, barter, or plunder, without so much as a peep of objection from the God in whose name these atrocities are committed. One woman, a concubine of a Levite man, is thrown to a mob, gang-raped, and dismembered as part of an intertribal dispute (Judges 19). Another young girl is ceremonially sacrificed to God after God grants a military victory to her father, Jephthah, who promised to offer as a burnt offering "whatever comes out of the door of my house to meet me when I return in triumph from the Ammonites" (Judges 11:31). Earlier, in the book of Numbers, God assists the Israelites in an attack against the Midianites, and tells the Israelites to kill every man, woman, and child from the community. They kill all except the young virgin girls whom the soldiers divide up as spoils of war. Feminist scholar Phyllis Trible aptly named these narratives "texts of terror."

"If art imitates life," she wrote, "scripture likewise reflects it in both holiness and horror."[2]

Rereading the texts of terror as a young woman, I kept anticipating some sort of postscript or epilogue chastising the major players for their sins, a sort of Arrested Development–style "lesson" to wrap it all up—*"And that's why you should always challenge the patriarchy!"* But no such epilogue exists. While women are raped, killed, and divided as plunder, God stands by, mute as clay.

I waited for a word from God, but no word came.

It was as though I lived suspended in the tension of two apparently competing convictions: that every human being is of infinite worth and value, and that the Bible is the infallible Word of God. These beliefs pulled at me with the gravitational forces of large planets. I couldn't get rid of them, and yet I couldn't seem to resolve them either. The tension was compounded by a growing confluence of misgivings I had about the absence of women in leadership in my church, the shaming of young women perceived to be immodest or "impure," and the insistence that God is most pleased when women are submissive and quiet. My home had always been a place of refuge, where the voices of women were valued and honored, but as I graduated from high school and entered college, I began to wonder if the same was true for the broader Christian community to which I belonged.

When I turned to pastors and professors for help, they urged me to set aside my objections, to simply trust that God is good and that the Bible's war stories happened as told, for reasons beyond my comprehension.

"God's ways are higher than our ways," they insisted. "Stop trying to know the mind of God."

It's an understandable approach. Human beings are finite and fallible, prone to self-delusion and sentimentality. If we rely exclusively on our feelings to guide us to truth, we are bound to get lost.

When asked in 2010 about Joshua's conquest of Canaan, Reformed pastor and theologian John Piper declared, without hesitation, "It's right for God to slaughter women and children anytime he pleases. God gives life and he takes life. Everybody who dies, dies because God wills that they die."[3]

Piper's dispassionate acceptance represented pure, committed faith, I was told, while mine had been infected by humanism and emotion—"a good example of why women should be kept from church leadership," one acquaintance said.

And for a moment, I believed it. For a moment, I felt silly for responding so emotionally to a bunch of old war stories that left the rest of the faithful seemingly unfazed. But this is the deleterious snare of fundamentalism: It claims that the heart is so corrupted by sin, it simply cannot be trusted to sort right from wrong, good from evil, divine from depraved. Instinct, intuition, conscience, critical thinking—these impulses must be set aside whenever they appear to contradict the biblical text, because the good Christian never questions the "clear teachings of Scripture"; the good Christian listens to God, not her gut.

I've watched people get so entangled in this snare they contort into shapes unrecognizable. When you can't trust your own God-given conscience to tell you what's right, or your own God-given mind to tell you what's true, you lose the capacity to engage the world in any meaningful, authentic way, and you become an easy target for authoritarian movements eager to exploit that vacuity for their gain. I tried reading Scripture with my conscience and curiosity suspended, and I felt, quite literally, disintegrated. I felt fractured and fake.

Brené Brown warned us we can't selectively numb our emotions, and no doubt this applies to the emotions we have about our faith.[4] If the slaughter of Canaanite children elicits only a shrug, then why not the slaughter of Pequots? Of Syrians? Of Jews? If we train ourselves not to ask hard questions about the Bible, and to emotionally distance ourselves from any potential conflicts or doubts, then where will we find the courage to challenge interpretations that justify injustice? How will we know when we've got it wrong?

"Belief in a cruel god makes a cruel man," Thomas Paine said.[5] If the Bible teaches that God is love, and love can look like genocide and violence and rape, then love can look like . . . *anything*. It's as much an invitation to moral relativism as you'll find anywhere.

I figured if God was real, then God didn't want the empty devotion of some shadow version of Rachel, but rather my whole, integrated self. So I decided to face the Bible's war stories head-on, mind and heart fully engaged, willing to risk the loss of faith if that's where the search led.

I listened to sermons. I read commentaries and theology books. I became a real downer at dinner parties:

"If you could travel anywhere in the world, where would you go?"
"Have you seen any of the Oscar-nominated films this year?"
"What's your Enneagram number?"
"Do you think God condones genocide?"

The explanations came hurried and certain. *Oh, God told Israel to wipe out the Canaanites because the Canaanites were super-duper evil, like the worst people ever. They worshipped idols and had orgies and sacrificed their children to their gods.*

So God condemned the practice of child sacrifice . . . by slaughtering children?

Well, that's just how things were back then. It was kill or be killed, tribal warfare and all that. Israel did what it had to do to survive.

Yes, but Israel was the aggressor in these stories. Joshua's armies weren't defending their land and their homes from foreign invaders; they *were* the foreign invaders.

What's the big deal? God sends millions of people to hell forever and is still a good God. The Canaanites were simply "vessels of wrath,

prepared for destruction," as Saint Paul puts it. You should just be grate-
ful you've been chosen for heaven. Stop worrying about everyone else.

That doesn't help. *At all.*

I began to feel a bit like the disheveled Berenger, a character from Eugène Ionesco's play *Rhinoceros,* who grows increasingly bewildered as the people of his provincial French town acclimate to the sudden presence of rhinoceroses in their community. In one scene, a rhinoceros thunders through the town square, trampling a housecat. After their initial shock, the villagers get sidetracked debating whether the rhino had one horn or two, and whether its origins are Asiatic or African. And on it goes throughout the play, as the townspeople themselves transform into rhinos, one by one, arguing all the while over pointless trivialities, until only Berenger remains human.

The play is about fascism, I think, but it reminds me a bit of Christians and their Bibles. Sometimes it seems as if there are all these rhinoceroses barreling through the pages of Scripture, pooping on sidewalks and flattening housecats, but we've grown so accustomed to defending their presence we end up debating the length of their tails.

A lot of people think the hardest part about religious doubt is feeling isolated from God. It's not. At least in my experience, the hardest part about doubt is feeling isolated from your community. There's nothing quite like going through the motions of Christian life—attending church, leading Bible study, singing hymns, bringing your famous lemon bars to potlucks—while internally questioning the very beliefs that hold the entire culture together. It's like you've got this ticker scrolling across every scene of your life, feeding you questions and commentary and doubts, and yet you carry on as though you can't see it, as if everything's fine. Say something and you risk losing friendships and becoming the subject of gossip. Keep your doubts to yourself and you risk faking it for the rest of your life. I know a lot of people, including some pastors, who are faking it.

At the crux of the dilemma hangs a single, haunting question: *If I belong to this community because I share its beliefs, what happens if I stop believing?* The threat of exile has a way of making those justifications for biblical genocide a lot easier to swallow.

My questions came with consequences. We left the church in which I was raised, and rumors of my "rebellious spirit" circulated around town, prompting more than a few well-meaning *interventions.* (Warning: Do not be lured by the promise of homemade chocolate chip cookies at a meeting to discuss "recent turns in your faith journey." It's a trap.) Friends stopped calling—both because of their own fears and because I pushed too hard to try and make them understand. And the doubts stuck around; they remain with me to this day.

But accepting the Bible's war stories without objection threatened to erase my humanity. "We don't become more spiritual by becoming less human," Eugene Peterson said.[6] How could I love God with all my heart, soul, mind, and strength while disengaging those very faculties every time I read the Bible?

So I brought my whole self into the wilderness with God—no faking, no halfway. And there we wrestled.

ᕱ

I've never liked war stories. *The Red Badge of Courage* was the first school reading assignment to bore me to tears, and I'm the only person I know over the age of twenty who hasn't seen *Saving Private Ryan* or *Apocalypse Now.* Civil War reenactments, common in this part of the South, give me the creeps, and most of what I've seen of *Game of Thrones* I've watched through my fingers while pleading,

"Is it over yet?" In my sole attempt at playing one of those single-shooter video games we progressives like to blame everything on, my character ran in a circle for five minutes before blowing itself up with a grenade.

But you don't have to like war stories to be profoundly influenced by them, and living in a country that spends more on its military than any other means I too am immersed in the imagery and rhetoric of war, no matter how sanitized I prefer it. From poems that immortalize revolutions in couplets, to viral videos of soldiers arriving home to their families, few narratives have as much influence over a culture's identity than the legends of its most famous military battles and heroes. Our war stories tell us where we come from, what we value, who we fear, and what we hate. They haunt our literature, our art, our monument-dotted landscapes. Generals historic and mythic have rallied their troops with the promise of being immortalized in the war stories of future generations. The famous Saint Crispin's Day Speech from Shakespeare's *Henry V*—"This story shall the good man teach his son / And Crispin Crispian shall ne'er go by / From this day to the ending of the world / But we in it shall be remembered"—finds echoes in Lin-Manuel Miranda's *Hamilton* lyrics, "The Story of Tonight."[7] Churchill made a similar appeal in a speech to the House of Commons at the start of World War II: "Let us therefore brace ourselves to our duties, and so bear ourselves that, if the British Empire and its Commonwealth last for a thousand years, men will still say, 'This was their finest hour.'"[8]

People take extraordinary risks to be part of a story that will outlive them.

Sometimes our stories glorify war. Sometimes they lament it. Traditionally they employ exaggerated rhetoric, ranging from a little hyperbole and creative license to shameless propaganda, with all sorts of iterations in between. Sometimes the details of a battle are well preserved by journalists or historians, but more often than not, they get distorted—by the shame of loss, by the pride of victory, by the new politics of a new age, or by the warped lens of time. If you really want to understand what makes a community or a culture tick, ask the people in it what they believe is worth dying for, or perhaps more significantly, worth killing for. Ask the people for their war stories.

Ancient Israel was no different. By the time many of the Bible's war stories were written down, several generations had passed, and Israel had evolved from a scrappy band of nomads living in the shadows of Babylon, Egypt, and Assyria to a nation that could hold its own, complete with a monarchy. Scripture embraces that underdog status in order to credit God with Israel's success and to remind a new generation that "some trust in chariots and some in horses, but we trust in the name of the LORD our God" (Psalm 20:7). The story of David and Goliath, in which a shepherd boy takes down one of those legendary Canaanite giants with just a slingshot and two stones, epitomizes Israel's self-understanding as a humble people improbably beloved, victorious only by the grace and favor of a God who rescued them from Egypt, walked with them through the desert, brought the walls of Jericho down, and made that shepherd boy a king.

To reinforce the miraculous nature of Israel's victories, the writers of Joshua and Judges describe forces of hundreds defeating armies of thousands with epic totality. These numbers are likely exaggerated and, in keeping literary conventions of the day, rely more on drama and bravado than the straightforward recitation of fact. Those of us troubled by language about the "extermination" of Canaanite populations may find some comfort in the fact that scholars and archaeologists doubt the early skirmishes of Israel's history actually resulted in genocide. It was common for warring tribes in ancient

Mesopotamia to refer to decisive victories as "complete annihilation" or "total destruction," even when their enemies lived to fight another day. (The Moabites, for example, claimed in an extrabiblical text that after their victory in a battle against an Israelite army, the nation of Israel "utterly perished for always," which obviously isn't the case. And even in Scripture itself, stories of conflicts with Canaanite tribes persist through the book of Judges and into Israel's monarchy, which would suggest Joshua's armies did not in fact wipe them from the face of the earth, at least not in a literal sense.)[9]

Theologian Paul Copan called it "the language of conventional warfare rhetoric," which "the knowing ancient Near Eastern reader recognized as hyperbole."[10]

Pastor and author of *The Skeletons in God's Closet*, Joshua Ryan Butler, dubbed it "ancient trash talk."[11]

Even Jericho, which twenty-first-century readers like to imagine as a colorful, bustling city with walls that reached the sky, was in actuality a small, six-acre military outpost, unlikely to support many civilians but, as was common, included a prostitute and her family. Most of the "cities" described in the book of Joshua were likely the same. So, like every culture before and after, Israel told its war stories with flourish, using the language and literary conventions that best advanced the agendas of storytellers.

As Peter Enns explained, for the biblical writers, "Writing about the past was never simply about understanding the past for its own sake, but about shaping, molding and creating the past to speak to the present."

"The Bible looks the way it does," he concluded, "because God lets his children tell the story."[12]

You see the children's fingerprints all over the pages of Scripture, from its origin stories to its deliverance narratives to its tales of land, war, and monarchy.

For example, as the Bible moves from conquest to settlement, we encounter two markedly different accounts of the lives of Kings Saul, David, and Solomon and the friends and enemies who shaped their reigns. The first appears in 1 and 2 Samuel and 1 and 2 Kings. These books include all the unflattering details of kingdom politics, including the account of how King David had a man killed so he could take the man's wife, Bathsheba, for himself. On the other hand, 1 and 2 Chronicles omit the story of David and Bathsheba altogether, along with much of the unseemly violence and drama around the transition of power between David and Solomon. This is because Samuel and Kings were likely written during the Babylonian exile, when the people of Israel were struggling to understand what they had done wrong for God to allow their enemies to overtake them, and 1 and 2 Chronicles were composed much later, after the Jews had returned to the land, eager to pick up the pieces. While the authors of Samuel and Kings viewed the monarchy as a morality tale to help them understand their present circumstances, the authors of the Chronicles recalled the monarchy with nostalgia, a reminder of their connection to God's anointed as they sought healing and unity. As a result, you get two noticeably different takes on the very same historic events.

In other words, the authors of Scripture, like the authors of any other work (including this one!), wrote with agendas. They wrote for a specific audience from a specific religious, social, and political context, and thus made creative decisions based on that audience and context.

Of course, this raises some important questions, like: Can war stories be inspired? Can political propaganda be God-breathed? To what degree did the Spirit guide the preservation of these narratives, and is there something sacred to be uncovered beneath all these human fingerprints?

I don't know the answers to all these questions, but I do know a few things.

The first is that not every character in these violent stories stuck with the script. After Jephthah sacrificed his daughter as a burnt offering in exchange for God's aid in battle, the young women of Israel engaged in a public act of grief marking the injustice. The text reports, "From this comes the Israelite tradition that each year the young women of Israel go out for four days to commemorate the daughter of Jephthah" (Judges 11:39–40). While the men moved on to fight another battle, the women stopped to acknowledge that something terrible had happened here, and with what little social and political power they had, they protested—every year for four days. They refused to let the nation forget what it had done in God's name. In another story, a woman named Rizpah, one of King Saul's concubines, suffered the full force of the monarchy's cruelty when King David agreed to hand over two of her sons to be hanged by the Gibeonites in an effort to settle a long, bloody dispute between the factions believed to be the cause of widespread famine across the land. A sort of biblical Antigone, Rizpah guarded her sons' bodies from birds and wild beasts for weeks, until at last the rain came and they could be buried. Word of her tragic stand spread across the kingdom and inspired David to pause to grieve the violence his house had wrought (2 Samuel 21). Even the prophetess Deborah, herself a legendary warrior, included in her victory song an acknowledgment of the defeated general's mother, whom Deborah imagined peering from the lattice of her window as she awaited her son's return, wondering, "Why is his chariot so long in coming? Why is the clatter of his chariots delayed?" (Judges 5:28). Deborah's portrait of the enemy is far from sympathetic—it reads more like a taunt, really—but it nevertheless broadens the narrative scope of the typical biblical war story to include the experiences of women.

The point is, if you pay attention to the women, a more complex history of Israel's conquests emerges. Their stories invite the reader to consider the human cost of violence and patriarchy, and in that sense prove instructive to all who wish to work for a better world. Of the Bible's texts of terror, theology professor and poet Nicola Slee wrote, "We will listen, however painful the hearing . . . until there is not one last woman remaining who is a victim of violence."[13] It's not always clear what we are meant to learn from the Bible's most troubling stories, but if we simply look away, we learn nothing.

In one of the most moving spiritual exercises of my adult faith, an artist friend and I created a liturgy of lament honoring the victims of the texts of terror. On a chilly December evening, we sat around the coffee table in my living room and lit candles in memory of Hagar, Jephthah's daughter, the concubine from Judges 19, and Tamar, the daughter of King David who was raped by her half brother. We read their stories, along with poetry and reflections composed by modern-day women who have survived gender-based violence. My friend built a diorama out of a pinewood box that featured five faceless wooden figures, huddled together beneath a ring of barbed wire, their silhouettes reflected on the backboard by pages cut from a book. Across the top of the box were printed the words of Christ—"As you have done unto the least of these, so you have done to me."

I recount the experience in my book *A Year of Biblical Womanhood*, and have since connected with pastors and worship leaders who have incorporated similar liturgies into their services, often during the season of Lent, when, among other things, Christians remember and repent of all evil done in God's name. Once, when I was speaking as a guest at a church in the Midwest, someone had arranged and lit five candles on the altar, four in honor of the biblical women we commemorated in our ceremony, and one in honor of all the women, past and present, who share in the sad solidarity of their suffering. The gesture moved me to tears.

If the Bible's texts of terror compel us to face with fresh horror and resolve the ongoing oppression and exploitation of women, then perhaps these stories do not trouble us in vain. Perhaps we can use them for some good.

The second thing I know is that we are not as different from the ancient Israelites as we would like to believe. "It was a violent and tribal culture," people like to say of ancient Israel to explain away its actions in Canaan. But, as Joshua Ryan Butler astutely observed, when it comes to civilian casualties, "we tend to hold the ancients to a much higher standard than we hold ourselves."[14] In the time it took me to write this chapter, nearly one thousand civilians were killed in airstrikes in Iraq and Syria, many of them women and children. The atomic bombs dropped on Hiroshima and Nagasaki took hundreds of thousands of lives in World War II, and far more civilians died in the Korean War and Vietnam War than American soldiers. Even though America is one of the wealthiest countries in the world, it takes in less than half of 1 percent of the world's refugees, and drone warfare has left many thousands of families across the Middle East terrorized.[15] This is not to excuse Israel's violence, because modern-day violence is also bad, nor is it to trivialize debates over just war theory and US involvement in various historical conflicts, which are complex issues far beyond the scope of this book. Rather, it ought to challenge us to engage the Bible's war stories with a bit more humility and intro-spection, willing to channel some of our horror over atrocities past into questioning elements of the war machines that still roll on today.

Finally, the last thing I know is this: If the God of the Bible is true, and if God became flesh and blood in the person of Jesus Christ, and if Jesus Christ is—as theologian Greg Boyd put it—"the revelation that culminates and supersedes all others,"[16] then God would rather die by violence than commit it. The cross makes this plain. On the cross, Christ not only bore the brunt of human cruelty and bloodlust and fear, he remained faithful to the nonviolence he taught and modeled throughout his ministry. Boyd called it "the Crucifixion of the Warrior God," and in a two-volume work by that name asserted that "on the cross, the diabolic violent warrior god we have all-too-frequently pledged allegiance to has been forever repudiated."[17] On the cross, Jesus chose to align himself with victims of suffering rather than the inflictors of it.

At the heart of the doctrine of the incarnation is the stunning claim that Jesus is what God is like. "No one has ever seen God," declared John in his gospel, "but the one and only Son, who is himself God and is in closest relationship with the Father, *has made him known*" (John 1:18, emphasis added). The New American Standard Bible says, "The only begotten God who is in the bosom of the Father, *He has explained Him*" (emphasis added). So to whatever extent God owes us an explanation for the Bible's war stories, Jesus is that explanation. And Christ the King won his kingdom without war.

The oldest hymn of the church puts a new spin on the traditional war ballad. In it the Christian sings of Jesus:

> Who, being in very nature God,
>> did not consider equality with God something to be used
>>> to his own advantage;
>> rather, he made himself nothing
>>> by taking the very nature of a servant,
>>> being made in human likeness.
> And being found in appearance as a man,
>> he humbled himself
>>> by becoming obedient to death—
>>> even death on a cross!

Therefore God exalted him to the highest place
and gave him the name that is above every name,
that at the name of Jesus every knee should bow,
in heaven and on earth and under the earth,
and every tongue acknowledge that Jesus Christ is Lord,
to the glory of God the Father.

(PHILIPPIANS 2:6–11)

Citing this hymn, the apostle Paul instructed Christians to "have this attitude in yourselves which was also in Christ Jesus" (2:5 NASB).

Jesus turned the war story on its head. Instead of being born to nobility, he was born in a manger, to an oppressed people in occupied territory. Instead of charging into Jerusalem on a warhorse, he arrived on a lumbering donkey. Instead of rallying troops for battle, he washed his disciples' feet. According to the apostle Paul, these are the tales followers of Jesus should be telling—with our words, with our art, and with our lives.

Of course, this still leaves us to grapple with the competing biblical portraits of God as the instigator of violence and God as the repudiator of violence. Boyd argued that God serves as a sort of "heavenly missionary" who temporarily accommodates the brutal practices and beliefs of various cultures without condoning them in order to gradually influence God's people toward justice. Insofar as any divine portrait reflects a character at odds with the cross, he said, it must be considered accommodation.[18] It's an interesting theory, though I confess I'm only halfway through Boyd's 1,492 pages, so I've yet to fully consider it. (I know I can't read my way out of this dilemma, but that won't keep me from trying.)

The truth is, I've yet to find an explanation for the Bible's war stories that I find completely satisfying. If we view this through

Occam's razor and choose the simplest solution to the problem, we might conclude that the ancient Israelites invented a deity to justify their conquests and keep their people in line. As such, then, the Bible isn't a holy book with human fingerprints; it's an entirely human construction, responsible for more vice than virtue.

There are days when that's what I believe, days when I mumble through the hymns and creeds at church because I'm not convinced they say anything true. And then there are days when the Bible pulls me back with a numinous force I can only regard as divine, days when Hagar and Deborah and Rahab reach out from the page, grab me by the face, and say, "Pay attention. This is for you."

I'm in no rush to patch up these questions. God save me from the day when stories of violence, rape, and ethnic cleansing inspire within me anything other than revulsion. I don't want to become a person who is unbothered by these texts, and if Jesus is who he says he is, then I don't think he wants me to be either. There are parts of the Bible that inspire, parts that perplex, and parts that leave you with an open wound. I'm still wrestling, and like Jacob, I will wrestle until I am blessed. God hasn't let go of me yet.

War is a dreadful and storied part of the human experience, and Scripture captures many shades of it—from the chest-thumping of the victors to the anguished cries of victims. There is ammunition there for those seeking religious justification for violence, and solidarity for all the mothers like Rizpah who just want an end to it. For those of us who prefer to keep the realities of war at a safe, sanitized distance, and who enjoy the luxury of that choice, the Bible's war stories force a confrontation with the darkness.

Maybe that's not such a bad thing.

THE DEBATE

(A Screenplay)

INT. Cafeteria—Day

Red plastic trays glide down the food bar. We watch from ABOVE as a pair of hands, shrink-wrapped in poly gloves and glowing with an ethereal light, pass steaming plates of today's special under the sneeze guard. Mashed potatoes and mystery meat. We hear the familiar, convivial din of CLINKING SILVERWARE and DISTANT CONVERSATION.

Cut To:

A long table, sparse and utilitarian, with nine seats on each side—
all empty, save one.

JOB, midthirties, sits alone at the center. He stares blankly at his food, shoulders slumped. His oxford and tweed fit the profile of a professor—humanities, judging by the absence of a tie—but his matted hair and three-day growth could get him mistaken for a hungover student. On the wall behind him, a smattering of fliers advertise sorority balls, lectures, and cheap apartments. An inspirational poster features a calico kitten hanging precariously from a tree limb. "Hang in there!" it says.

Coeds pass in front of the table, lost in chatter. A WOMAN with an armful of papers to grade walks briskly toward the table, heels assaulting the floor, but the minute she spots Job, she freezes, then does an about-face to *clop, clop, clop* away. Job doesn't notice.

More coeds pass by, until finally ELI approaches the table with a tray in his hands and sits down cautiously next to Job. They are close in age, but Eli's beard is obviously intentional, the sort of extracurricular activity he brags about in his faculty bio, along with his interest in foreign films and craft beer. Eli takes Job in. He starts to speak, then thinks better of it, poking at his mystery meat instead.

The two sit in silence until BILL arrives with a paper bag lunch and takes the seat on the other side of Job. Bill, late sixties, has the wizened air of a longtime professor who has survived his fair share of inept administrations. He nods a greeting to Eli, who returns it, then to Job, who does not. He pulls out a peanut butter sandwich and takes a bite, content with the quiet.

FATHER Z is the last to arrive, having walked from the divinity school. The fiftysomething wears a collar under his blazer and carries a plastic container of mixed greens and a plastic fork. Before sitting, he rests his hand for a moment on Job's shoulder, as if to offer a prayer. No reaction from Job. Father Z takes the seat next to Bill so the four colleagues form a single outward-facing row, a sad little tableau. No one sits across from them.

Finally, the silence becomes too much for Eli. He pulls a greeting card from his jacket. It says "With Sympathy" on the front. No envelope.

Eli

We got this for you, man. It's not much, I know, but under the circumstances, we just . . . we wanted to do something.

Job wakes from his stupor, takes the card, and opens it.

Job
(reading the card, deadpan)

Remember, God will never give you more than you can handle.

He puts the card on the table and falls back into a daze. Eli seems satisfied, but Bill makes a face.

Eli
(to Bill)

What? What's wrong with the card?

Bill

It's a tad cliché, don't you think? "God will never give you more than you can handle"? What's that even mean?

Eli

It's just a card, Bill. It's not a theological statement.

Bill

Everything's a theological statement. You of all people should know that.

Bill looks to Father Z for support, but Father Z keeps his eyes on his salad.

Eli considers Bill's challenge for a moment. He has to lean over Job to resume the conversation with his colleagues.

Eli
(lowering voice)

Look, this obviously happened for a reason. We know God is in control and that there is some divine purpose at work here. We don't need to spell that out for Job; he gets it. I figured a few words of comfort would encourage him to consider what he might learn from this time of discipline. Blessed is the one whom God corrects, so do not despise the discipline of the Almighty. For he wounds, but he also binds up; he injures, but his hands also heal.

Bill

Well, that would have been a much better way to put it.

The friends fall silent for a moment, all of them eating except for Job. We hear only the CLINK of flatware on plates and the distant HUM of less-awkward conversations, until Bill can no longer keep his opinion to himself. He puts down his sandwich.

Bill

Really, this should serve as a reminder that we're all just one sin away from similar judgment. If anything, we ought to be urging Job to repent so God will show mercy.

(to Job)

You know, if you seek God earnestly and plead with the Almighty, if you are pure and upright, even now he will rouse himself on your behalf.

Job doesn't respond. Bill returns to his sandwich, glad he got that off his chest.

Eli
(to Bill)

Of what should Job repent? Specific sins?

Bill

Aren't all sins specific, Eli?

Eli

Well, sure. I guess I'm asking if you think Job did something definitive to bring this on or if it's more, like, a result of God's wrath on his general sinful state. You said it could happen to any of us . . .

Bill

Yeah, but it didn't happen to any of us. It happened to Job.

Eli

Right, but why?

Bill

Pride. Greed. Sloth.

Eli

I've not seen Job exhibit any of those qualities. I mean, we all know him to be a man of—

Bill

Porn.

Eli

Porn? Oh good grief, Bill. It always comes back to porn with you. You really think God's so enraged Job got a peek at some boobs online, he sends a rainstorm and a drunk driver to the very road where . . .

An excruciating pause.

Eli
(*to Job*)

Oh, God. I'm sorry, dude. I'm so sorry.

Bill
(*matter-of-fact*)

God rewards the righteous and punishes evildoers. The Writings are clear on that. Does God pervert justice? Does the Almighty pervert what is right? Certainly not. Whatever the sin, it was severe enough to warrant correction. We have to trust that God is just.

Eli knows he should let it go, but he just can't let Bill have the final word.

Eli

I agree, Bill. But it doesn't have to be direct cause and effect. I think it's entirely possible this was a result of God's general anger toward sin, like with the earthquake a few weeks ago or the famine over in Sudan, not necessarily a direct effect of Job's porn addiction.

Father Z

Job has a porn addiction?

Eli

According to Bill, everyone has a porn addiction.

Bill

Yep. Because of feminism.

Eli

(*to Bill*)

All I'm saying is, I think it's entirely possible God did this to discipline Job's sins in general, not one sin in particular, which should sober us all. Hardship does not spring from the soil, nor does trouble sprout from the ground. Yet man is born to trouble as surely as sparks fly upward.

Father Z

I don't think Job's convinced he's guilty of anything.

At this, everyone at the table turns to Father Z, and then to Job. Job looks back at Father Z, as though suddenly seeing a stranger or trying to read a sign in a different language.

Job

What?

Father Z

Do you think you are blameless, Job?

Job

I . . . I don't know . . . Blameless? . . . I . . .

Father Z

Do you recognize this as an opportunity for repentance?

Job struggles, then finally answers, tentatively.

Job

No. Not really.

Father Z

Well, I'm sorry to hear that.

Job

I don't think I've done anything wrong, Father.

Father Z

(*in preacher mode*)

Oh, how I wish that God would speak, that he would open his lips against you and disclose to you the secrets of wisdom! He has already overlooked so much of your sin, Job; how can you claim to be blameless? If God confines you in prison and convenes a court, who can oppose him? You must repent, brother, and turn your heart to him. Put away your sins, and God will work this out for good.

He pauses for dramatic effect.

Father Z

. . . Yes, even *this* can be redeemed for good.

The group absorbs Father Z's sermon. Job puts his head in his hands. He wears a wedding ring.

Bill, not to be outdone, tries one more point.

Bill

I think we should consider that maybe this isn't just about Job's sins, but the sins of the ones actually in the accident.

At this, Job lifts his head from his hands to look at Bill, and for the first time we catch a glimmer of emotion—utter anguish.

Suddenly, everything stops. Complete silence. All the background clamor ceases, as if someone has hit a mute button on the cafeteria. The fluorescent lights above the table throb, glowing brighter and brighter, until nearly everything is blown out. The professors, startled, squint and shield their eyes.

The silhouette of a CAFETERIA LADY moves imposingly into the frame. She wears a hairnet and apron. Her hands, shrink-wrapped in poly gloves, rest on her hips.

Cafeteria Lady

Enough! Enough with this!

She speaks with a thick Latin accent.

Cafeteria Lady

Stop lying about me, you fools. You think because you've got a bunch of fancy theology degrees, you can divine what I'm up to? Who keeps the earth spinning in her orbit and knows every dimension of the cosmos, huh? Who formed galaxies out of dark matter and brought life out of the sea? Who knows every strand of DNA in every plant and every animal and every person in the world? And who is acquainted with every human sorrow, from the tears of a child to the groans of slaves? Who can fathom the depths of the ocean? Who can start or stop the rain? Who knows, intimately, the contents of every human heart?

She waits.

Cafeteria Lady

That's right. NOT. YOU. So lay off my servant Job. He hasn't done anything wrong. He is blameless and upright, a man of kindness and integrity, which is more than I can say for the three of you.

Stunned, the professors sit with mouths agape until Bill attempts to speak. He moves his mouth, but no sound comes out. Same with Eli and Father Z. The three enter into a frantic, soundless "conversation" as Job rises to his feet, tears streaming down his face.

Cafeteria Lady

C'mon, Job. I know you've got some things to get off your chest.

She walks out of frame. Job follows with reckless abandon, nearly falling over his chair to get to her.

The lights return to normal. The CAFETERIA SOUNDS resume. But the three professors continue arguing without voices, employing dramatic gestures to compensate.

At the center of it all sits an empty chair.

Fade to Black

4

WISDOM STORIES

Live a righteous life and you will prosper. Live an unrighteous one and you will suffer.

It's a simple conceit, and a common one throughout Scripture.

"Trouble pursues the sinner," says Proverbs 13:21, "but the righteous are rewarded with good things."

"The righteous eat to their hearts' content," says verse 25, "but the stomach of the wicked goes hungry."

"A little while, and the wicked will be no more," declares the psalmist. "But the meek will inherit the land and enjoy peace and prosperity" (Psalm 37:10–11).

For the people of Israel, this principle of reward and punishment was established in the beginning, when God gave their ancestors the Ten Commandments and told them to "walk in obedience to all that the LORD your God has commanded you, so that you may live and prosper and prolong your days in the land that you will possess" (Deuteronomy 5:33). Sure enough, when Joshua followed God's instructions, Israel won its battles; when even a single soldier strayed, its armies faltered. The people watched as their leaders suffered the consequences of disobedience. Saul lost his crown, David four of his sons, Solomon his kingdom. The prophets believed even the Babylonian exile to be divine punishment for Israel's transgressions, an indictment on the nation's greed, idolatry, and neglect of the poor. The connection between suffering and sin remained pervasive enough in first-century Jewish thought that when Jesus' disciples encountered a man blind from birth, they asked their Rabbi, "Who sinned, this man or his parents, that he was born blind?" (John 9:2).

So it's understandable how a superficial reading of Scripture might lead someone to conclude that it teaches a sort of karmic reciprocity between God and people, wherein those who behave honorably and keep the commandments are blessed, while those who lie, cheat, and steal get their comeuppance.

But that only captures half the conversation.

Enter Job.

Job did everything right. The eighteenth book of the Bible describes its eponymous hero as "blameless and upright," a man who "feared God and shunned evil" (1:1). Job was faithful to his wife, kind to the poor, and generous with his workers. A wealthy landowner boasting many thousands of sheep, camels, and oxen, he had ten beloved children and regularly made burnt offerings to God on their behalf. In fact, Job maintained such a virtuous lifestyle it drew the attention of God, who, in one of the Bible's most imaginative and confounding scenes, makes a wager with Satan that Job would remain faithful even if he lost everything. As a result of this wager, Job's livestock and servants are destroyed by enemies, his fields are consumed by fire, and his children are killed when a freak windstorm collapses their tent—*all in one day*. But even after Job is himself stricken with terrible sores that leave him scratching at his body with a shard of broken pottery, he refuses to curse God. Instead, he shaves his head, tears his clothes, and sings:

> "Naked I came from my mother's womb,
>   and naked I will depart.
> The LORD gave and the LORD has taken away;
>   may the name of the LORD be praised." (1:21)

As he grieves in a heap of ashes outside the city, Job is visited by three of his friends—Eliphaz, Bildad, and Zophar (or, if you like, Eli, Bill, and Father Z). For seven days and seven nights they sit with him in silence in an act of solidarity Jewish readers will recognize as "sitting shiva." But when Job cries out in agony to curse the day he was born, Eliphaz can't help but respond, delivering a monologue about how Job must have sinned to incite this tragedy, for, "Who, being innocent, has ever perished? Where were the upright ever destroyed?" (4:7).

"As I have observed," Eliphaz says, repeating an ancient idiom that has survived to this day, "those who plow evil and those who sow trouble reap it" (v. 8).

In other words, "You reap what you sow."

What follows is a series of speeches and responses in which the cause of Job's suffering and the nature of wisdom are hotly debated. This discussion consumes the bulk of the book's forty-nine chapters and includes some of Scripture's most lyrical refrains. Indeed, lines from the speeches of Eliphaz, Bildad, and Zophar could easily be mistaken for lines from the book of Psalms or Proverbs:

> Submit to God and be at peace with him;
>   in this way prosperity will come to you.
>
>   (22:21)

Blessed is the one whom God corrects;
    so do not despise the discipline of the Almighty.
For he wounds, but he also binds up;
    he injures, but his hands also heal.

        (5:17–18)

Can you fathom the mysteries of God?
    Can you probe the limits of the Almighty?
They are higher than the heavens above—what can you do?
    They are deeper than the depths below—what can you
        know?
Their measure is longer than the earth
    and wider than the sea.

        (11:7–9)

Yet Job is anything but comforted by the words of his friends.

"You are miserable comforters, all of you!" he cries. "Will your long-winded speeches never end?" (16:2–3).

In spite of their accusations and pontifications, Job maintains his innocence. He speaks plainly about his pain, confusion, and disillusionment with God. He begs God for an explanation.

Finally, after thirty-seven chapters of speeches, God talks back, and in a voice thundering from a whirlwind, demands, "Where were you when I laid the earth's foundation? Tell me, if you understand. . . . Have you ever given orders to the morning, or shown the dawn its place?" (38:4, 12).

Then, in some of the most beautiful poetry from the ancient world, the author of Job enumerates, with both breathtaking scope and rich particularity, the work of God throughout the universe—from God's sovereignty over the moon and stars, thunder and snow, dewdrops and ocean waves, to God's utter delight in the crowing of the rooster, the birth of baby mountain goats, the freedom of the wild donkey, and the flapping of ostrich wings. God knows the path of the planets and the direction of every lightning strike, the text declares. God can snag a sea monster with a fishhook, "bind the chains of the Pleiades," and "loosen Orion's belt" (38:31). Even the earth's most frightening untamed creature, the reptilian Leviathan, is beloved by its Creator, each of its scales set in place with the same lapidary care that fashioned Job in his mother's womb.

It's not exactly a straightforward answer to the issue of theodicy (why God allows suffering and evil to persist in the world), but it's a striking one that expands the question of causality to include the furthest reaches of the universe and the minuscule barbs of an ostrich feather.

After this poetic tour of the cosmos, God rebukes Job's friends for not speaking the truth as Job has, and instructs them to make offerings as penance. In a rather satisfying final burn, God informs the three philosophers that Job, the man they had condemned as a sinner, will have to intercede in prayer on their behalf, "and I will accept his prayer and not deal with you according to your folly" (42:8).

Job's health is restored, his wealth doubled. He has ten more children and dies at the age of 140, "full of years" (v. 17). God never tells Job about that wager with the Devil.

No one doubts the literary achievement of the book of Job, its imagery and themes influencing everything from Handel's *Messiah* to Joseph Stein's *Fiddler on the Roof* to Dostoyevsky's *The Brothers Karamazov*. But identifying the genre of the original story can be tricky. Some call it a folktale, others a work of theological speculation. Tennyson called it "the greatest poem of ancient or modern times."[1] But most agree the book of Job falls squarely in the tradition of wisdom literature.

In the world of the ancient Near East, wisdom wasn't just

a virtue; it was a coveted commodity, prized for its promise of a full and honorable life. The book of Proverbs compares wisdom to rubies, gold, and silver, and claims "nothing you desire can compare with her" (Proverbs 3:15). And so the sages and wise men of the court were treated like rock stars as they instructed their disciples using pithy, easy-to-memorize maxims and riddles and debated among themselves the nature of truth, suffering, God, and the universe. Some of their surviving writings read as straightforward, practical, and worldly wise, while other pieces are more speculative and introspective, even pessimistic. In the Protestant Bible, the books of Job, Psalms, Proverbs, Ecclesiastes, and Song of Solomon are generally grouped together and categorized as wisdom literature. Jews identify these books as part of the Ketuvim, or "Writings"—miscellaneous works that are neither Torah nor prophecy.

Wisdom literature can take the form of short, didactic insights (as in the book of Proverbs), or poetry (as in the books of Psalms and Song of Solomon), or story and soliloquy (as in the books of Job and Ecclesiastes). The Bible's wisdom literature includes everything from admonitions against getting drunk to erotic poetry that would make E. L. James blush, to the ruminations of a wealthy sage suffering an existential crisis, to an acrostic poem extolling the virtues of an excellent wife. One of my favorite insights in all the Bible's wisdom literature comes from Proverbs 27:14: "If anyone loudly blesses their neighbor early in the morning, it will be taken as a curse."

As we say in the Episcopal Church, *this is the Word of the Lord.*

The aim of wisdom literature is to uncover something true about the nature of reality in a way that makes the reader or listener wiser. In the Bible, wisdom is rarely presented as a single decision, belief, or rule, but rather as a "way" or "path" that the sojourner must continually discern amid the twists and turns of life.

I had a college professor who assigned the book of Proverbs

to his Psychology 101 class, instructing us to circle in our Bibles every appearance of the word *way* or *path*. The point, he said, is that wisdom isn't about sticking to a set of rules or hitting some imaginary bull's-eye representing "God's will." Wisdom is a way of life, a journey of humility and faithfulness we take together, one step at a time. To an anxious student who spent a lot of time worrying that her major or her homecoming date or her student senate bid were outside of God's will, this lesson proved an enormous comfort.

So what does the story of Job say about wisdom?

Well, for one thing, it favors the wisdom of those who have actually suffered over those who merely speculate about it.

"From this book above all others in scripture, we learn that the person in pain is a theologian of unique authority," wrote Old Testament scholar Ellen Davis in her marvelous book titled *Getting Involved with God*. "The one who complains to God, pleads with God, rails at God, does not let God off the hook for a minute—she is at last admitted to a mystery. She passes through a door that only pain will open, and is thus qualified to speak of God in a way that others, whom we generally call more fortunate, cannot speak."[2]

Even more significantly, the book of Job challenges the prevailing wisdom—wisdom found elsewhere in Scripture—that good things happen to good people and bad things happen to bad people. As professor and author Timothy Beal put it, "The book of Job is like a fault line running through the Bible. In it, the moral universe affirmed in texts like Deuteronomy, according to which righteousness equals blessed well-being and disobedience equals cursed suffering, is shaken to its core."[3]

But it's not just Job. Throughout the Bible's wisdom literature we catch pieces of *the other side of the conversation* regarding punishment and reward. The same psalmist who declares, "A little while and the wicked will be no more," elsewhere demands of God, "How long will you defend the unjust and show partiality to the wicked?" and describes in anguished detail the successes and pleasures of evil people, lamenting, "They are free from common human burdens; they are not plagued by human ills. . . . Surely in vain I have kept my heart pure and have washed my hands in innocence" (Psalms 37:10; 82:2; 73:5, 13). The author of Ecclesiastes simply argues, "When times are good, be happy; but when times are bad, consider this: God has made the one as well as the other" (Ecclesiastes 7:14).

In short, when it comes to the nature of suffering and blessing, the Bible does not speak with a single voice. There is not a biblical *view* of theodicy. There are biblical *views* of theodicy. And the people who wrote and assembled Scripture seemed perfectly fine with that unresolved tension.

Job's friends make the mistake of assuming that what is true in one context must be true in every context—a common error among modern Bible readers who like to trawl the text for universal answers. Eliphaz, Bildad, and Zophar said some "biblical" things in their remarks to Job, and yet in that context, those things weren't true. We should be wary, then, of grand pronouncements that begin, "The Bible says." *Where? To whom? In what context? Why?* "You reap what you sow" may apply in one circumstance, like when the apostle Paul said it in his letter to the Galatian church to encourage them to continue in good works (Galatians 6:7), but it fell woefully short in the context of Job's plight. So Job rightly condemns his friends-turned-accusers, saying, "If only you would be altogether silent! *For you that would be wisdom*" (13:5, emphasis added).

Wisdom, it seems, is situational. It isn't just about knowing what to say; it's about knowing when to say it. And it's not just about knowing *what* is true; it's about knowing *when* it's true.

You reap what you sow—except when you don't.

To engage the Bible with wisdom, then, is to embrace its diversity, not fight it. "For everything there is a season," wrote the sage of Ecclesiastes, ". . . a time to mourn, and a time to dance . . . a time to tear, and a time to sew, a time to keep silence, and a time to speak, a time to love, and a time to hate" (Ecclesiastes 3:1, 4, 7–8 ESV).

Arguably, these verses imply a pro tip too: When your friend is sitting in a heap of ashes, grieving the loss of his family and scratching his diseased skin with a shard of broken pottery, it's time to be silent. It's a time to listen and grieve.

German Jewish philosopher Theodor Adorno once said, "To let suffering speak is the condition of all truth."[4] If the Bible's war stories reveal the perils of letting God's children tell the story, then the Bible's wisdom stories uncover the beauty of it, the necessity. In the paradox of Job, the vulnerability of the Psalms, and the angst of Ecclesiastes, God's children are invited into the whirlwind, to cry out and question, to demand and debate, and to consider the big questions of life without resting in easy answers. The Bible reflects the complexity and diversity of the human experience, with all its joys and sorrows. And in the story of Job, it's not the learned theologians who get the peek at glory, but the man who said, with candor and courage, "I desire to argue with God."

ॐ

In many ways, the Bible of my youth was set up to fail. While American evangelicalism instilled in me a healthy love and respect for Scripture (without which this book would never have been written, I'm sure), many of its institutions taught me to expect something from the Bible that the Bible was never intended to deliver—namely, an internally consistent and self-evident worldview that provides clear, universal answers to all of life's questions, from whether climate change is real, to why God allows suffering in the world, to how to keep a marriage together and raise obedient kids. The Bible, I learned, served as a kind of owner's manual for life, *Basic Instructions Before Leaving Earth*. It came without flaws or contradictions and could be trusted to speak clearly and decisively on any political or social issue up for debate.

As a result, I emerged from my conservative Christian college with what I thought was the *biblical* view of American history, the *biblical* view of economics, the *biblical* view of gender and sexuality, the *biblical* view of science, the *biblical* view of politics, the *biblical* view of pop culture. The problem was, in most cases, the texts I memorized to support those views were selectively chosen to support a particular set of ideologies—usually politically conservative ones—a fact that became apparent when, after graduation, I encountered devoted Christians who believed and voted and worshipped quite differently than me, and could just as handily cite Scripture to support their points of view. As my exposure to science, travel, literature, and people of other faiths and backgrounds increased, many of the "biblical" positions I'd once held became emotionally and intellectually untenable. I realized, for example, that I'd been taught to formulate an entire economic philosophy around Paul's instructions to the Thessalonian church that "the one who is unwilling to work shall not eat" (2 Thessalonians 3:10) while setting aside hundreds of other biblical passages that call for economic justice for the poor, including those too disadvantaged to work. Volunteering at a local free health clinic, where I cried with patients enduring terrible, chronic pain because they couldn't afford their medication, upended for me the notion that the only *biblical* position on America's health care crisis was to leave it to the free market to solve. And when it came time to start my own family, all those "biblical principles for marriage" that crowned the husband the head of the home and restricted women's roles to homemaking and child care failed to fit the marriage I actually had, which functioned much more like a partnership than a hierarchy, and was healthier for it.

The owner's manual Bible, with its single prescriptions for all people in all circumstances, just didn't fit the complexities of actual life. Indeed, I know many people who suffered for years because they had been taught to rely on the Bible alone for help with depression, anxiety, or addiction when professional counseling and medication were also clearly necessary.

I'd always thought the more time I spent with the Bible, the more clarity I would receive, but as my nightstand grew cluttered with precarious stacks of books presenting *Four Views on Atonement*, *Three Views on Hell*, *Five Views on Evolution*, and *Four Views on Homosexuality*, it became apparent that, even among people who believed the Bible to speak with authority, the Bible's message is not always plain. The presence of hundreds, if not thousands, of Christian denominations makes this point obvious.

I had encountered what Catholic sociologist Christian Smith termed "pervasive interpretive pluralism," which simply refers to the reality that even among people devoted to its truth, the Bible yields different interpretations and applications of its many teachings. This reality challenges the idea that the Bible is a straightforward blueprint for living or a compendium of inerrant teachings on which the faithful will always agree.

"Even among presumably well-intentioned readers," Smith wrote in *The Bible Made Impossible*, ". . . the Bible, after their very best efforts to understand it, says and teaches very different things about most significant topics."[5]

While the Bible certainly presents recurring themes—like confession and repentance of sins, justice for the poor and oppressed, love for neighbor and hospitality to strangers—it's not always clear exactly how these themes should inform modern marriages or public policy or day-to-day decision-making. A book of poetry, stories, letters, and prophecies cannot be easily rendered down into bullet points, so treating Scripture as an owner's manual, based on a few verses here and a few verses there, will leave you more lost than found.

It's a bit like programming your GPS to take you to a destination, then ignoring every instinct in your body as its cheery voice tells you to take an exit you know you're not supposed to take or make a U-turn in the middle of a suspension bridge. There's a great episode of *The Office* in which this strategy lands Michael Scott and Dwight Schrute in a lake during a sales trip, Michael shouting, "The machine knows!" as he follows the GPS instructions and drives his SUV off the road into the water.

I've watched a lot of good people drive their lives, their families, their churches, their communities, even their countries into a lake, shouting, "The Bible knows!" all the way down.

The truth is, the Bible isn't an answer book. It's not even a book, really. Rather, it's a diverse library of ancient texts, spanning multiple centuries, genres, and cultures, authored by a host of different authors coming from a variety of different perspectives. These texts, like others from antiquity, have undergone edits, revisions, copies, and translations through the years. No one has the originals. Before they were canonized, they circulated as disparate collections of scrolls and codices, and before that, many were passed down as oral traditions. The Scripture Jesus knew and taught looked nothing like the specialty Bibles we sell in our Christian bookstores or even the giant, leather-bound heirlooms we treasure in our churches. Jews were still debating which texts should be canonized in their

Scripture a century after Jesus' death, and Christians were arguing over the shape of their canon well into the Protestant Reformation. (Luther wanted to leave out the book of James, for example, which he called "an epistle of straw.")[6]

Ask a Catholic monk, an Orthodox priest, an evangelical pastor, and a Reform rabbi how many books are in the Bible, and you'll get four different answers. These various traditions sort their books in different ways too, because Scripture consists of stories, poems, proverbs, letters, laws, genealogies, parables, and a host of other genres that can be difficult to categorize since they emerge from a culture so different from our own.

Because of all this, the Bible makes a lousy owner's manual. It fails massively at getting to the point. The Bible isn't some Magic 8 Ball you can consult when deciding whether to take a job or break up with a guy, nor is it a position paper elucidating God's opinion on various social, theological, and political issues. While we may wish for a clear, perspicuous text, that's not what God gave us. Instead, God gave us a cacophony of voices and perspectives, all in conversation with one another, representing the breadth and depth of the human experience in all its complexities and contradictions.

This inherent diversity is perhaps most obvious and most celebrated in the Bible's wisdom literature. While the book of Proverbs proclaims, "Get wisdom. Though it cost all you have, get understanding" (4:7), the author of Ecclesiastes posits, "With much wisdom comes much sorrow; the more knowledge, the more grief (1:18). "A cheerful heart is good medicine," says Proverbs 17:22, but Ecclesiastes 7:3 counters with "Frustration is better than laughter because a sad face is good for the heart." And lest you think all the tension lies between the perky Proverbs and her brooding little brother Ecclesiastes, consider these admonitions, which appear side by side in Proverbs 26:

> Do not answer a fool according to his folly, or you yourself will be just like him (v. 4). Answer a fool according to his folly, or he will be wise in his own eyes (v. 5).

I could list a dozen more from Psalms, Proverbs, and Ecclesiastes alone, but the point is, the Bible doesn't always agree with itself. As Timothy Beal put it, "The Bible canonizes contradiction."[7]

While these disparities may cause modern-day literalists to squirm, the authors and compilers of Scripture saw no need to iron them out. In fact, Jewish readers make a point of highlighting the Bible's contradictions to spark discussion and debate. The ancients were not so removed from the realities of actual life that they didn't realize wisdom and discernment are situational, that what may be wise in one context may be foolish in another.

When God gave us the Bible, God did not give us an internally consistent book of answers. God gave us an inspired library of diverse writings, rooted in a variety of contexts, that have stood the test of time, precisely because, together, they avoid simplistic solutions to complex problems. It's almost as though God trusts us to approach them with wisdom, to use discernment as we read and interpret, and to remain open to other points of view.

"The iconic idea of the Bible as a book of black-and-white answers," wrote Beal, "encourages us to remain in a state of spiritual immaturity. . . . In turning readers away from the struggle, from wrestling with the rich complexity of biblical literature and its history, in which there are no easy answers, it perpetuates an adolescent faith. It keeps us out of the deep end, where we have to 'ride these monsters down,' as Annie Dillard put it, trusting that it's not about the end product but the process."[8]

We see this adolescent faith manifested at times in the industry that produces Christian books, movies, music, and art, where well-intentioned creators like myself are often tempted to tell simplistic stories in service to our faith. The world has questions, we assume, so it's up to us to provide the answers. But this posture can easily result in heavy-handed, didactic work, designed to prop up ideologies rather than to capture the beauty and nuance of the actual human experience, which cannot be truthfully rendered with stereotypes or tidy endings. One popular Christian movie recently grossed more than $62 million by pitting an evil atheist professor against a heroic Christian student and forcing the atheist into an encounter with God by (spoiler alert!) running him over with a car, eliciting a deathbed conversion.

Contrast this with a film like *Philomena*, a quiet Oscar winner from 2013 and one of my favorite faith-themed movies of all time. *Philomena* traces the heartbreaking journey of a devout Irish woman (played by Judi Dench) who sets out to find her long-lost son, whom she was forced to give up for adoption as a teenager by nuns who kept her like a prisoner in a convent full of other unwed mothers in the 1950s. Her unlikely partner in this venture is a washed-up journalist named Martin Sixsmith (Steve Coogan), who reluctantly finds himself chronicling this "human interest story" while he waits for his reputation to be restored. The film's dialogue is smart and playful, its tone pitch-perfect. Dench masters her role as the provincial, inexperienced Philomena, who annoys the skeptical Martin with her old-fashioned sensibilities and penchant for lowbrow romance novels. The banter between the two alternates between hilarious and profound. In one scene, Philomena asks Martin if he believes in God, and in response he delivers a lengthy, anxious soliloquy about the impossibility of answering that question and the arrogance of certainty in the face of the unknown. When he asks Philomena the same question, she simply responds, "Yes."

But neither character is portrayed one-dimensionally. Both are imperfect, sympathetic, complicated, and surprising. Unlike all those caricatures that depict atheists as blindly antagonistic toward people of faith, Martin's frustrations with religion are reasonable and relatable, especially given the circumstances, and even after at least five viewings of the film, I find myself nodding along as he urges Philomena to confront the evil done to her by the church.

"I don't like that word, *evil*," responds Philomena.

"No, evil's good," the reporter assures her, "story-wise."

Yet time and again, Philomena confounds both Martin and the audience with a faith that is at once understated and brave, quiet and profound. In the end, the two come together in a powerful moment in which Martin, though he is justifiably angry and fed up with the abuses of the convent that betrayed Philomena, nevertheless purchases a gift for her from their gift shop, to be presented with love at one of her most vulnerable moments.

It's a careful, understated portrayal of the actual human experience, where clear-cut lines between good and evil, heroes and villains, right and wrong might be good "story-wise," for a newspaper headline but don't reflect the reality in which most people of faith actually live. It's unusual to find a movie in which one relates so sincerely to both the character of faith and the skeptic, but with *Philomena*, I did. The story simply rang true.

I believe that any time we tell stories like these that embrace complexity, we are participating in Scripture's wisdom tradition. We are doing the thing to which all artists are called, which is not to dazzle or instruct or lecture, but to tell the truth—in all its beauty, frustration, and surprise. We might not make $62 million at it, but we are, in the words of Proverbs, "walk[ing] in the way of insight" (Proverbs 9:6).

I love the challenge of creating like that. May I come to love the challenge of living like that too.

๛

How precious to me are your thoughts, God!
How vast is the sum of them!
Were I to count them,
they would outnumber the grains of sand . . .

Search me, God, and know my heart;
test me and know my anxious thoughts.
See if there is any offensive way in me,
and lead me in the way everlasting.

(PSALM 139:17–18, 23–24)

These words from Psalm 139 are some of my favorite from Scripture, and apparently I'm not alone. Often I see them printed on inspirational desk calendars and coffee mugs, and they remain a favorite in liturgy and worship across a diversity of denominations.

But Psalm 139 is almost always quoted selectively, for hiding after those conveniently placed ellipses lie these startling lines:

If only you, God, would slay the wicked!
Away from me, you who are bloodthirsty!
They speak of you with evil intent;
your adversaries misuse your name.
Do I not hate those who hate you, LORD,
and abhor those who are in rebellion against you?
I have nothing but hatred for them;
I count them my enemies.

(PSALM 139:19–22)

Not exactly greeting card material, is it?

The notion that they contain only uplifting words of comfort and praise is one of the most common misconceptions about the Bible's Psalms—a collection of 150 songs and poems that served as the hymnbook for postexilic Judaism and as the prayer book in many Judeo-Christian traditions to this day. While soaring exultations certainly make their mark ("Shout for joy to the LORD, all the earth!"), they appear side by side with lament ("I am worn out from my groaning. All night long I flood my bed with weeping and drench my couch with tears."), confession ("I know my transgressions, and my sin is always before me"), anger ("I cry out by day, but you do not answer"), and bold interrogations of the divine ("How long, LORD? Will you hide yourself forever?").[9] Because many of the Psalms were composed during the heartache and confusion of the Babylonian exile, they include gut-wrenching lamentations like Psalm 44, which says of God:

> You made us retreat before the enemy,
>> and our adversaries have plundered us.
> You gave us up to be devoured like sheep
>> and have scattered us among the nations.
> You sold your people for a pittance,
>> gaining nothing from their sale.

(VV. 10–12)

The Bible even includes what are sometimes called "cursing psalms," in which the author sings some pretty disturbing songs about his enemy:

> May his children be fatherless
>> and his wife a widow.

May his children be wandering beggars;

may they be driven from their ruined homes.

May a creditor seize all he has;

may strangers plunder the fruits of his labor.

May no one extend kindness to him

or take pity on his fatherless children.

(PSALM 109:9–12)

If the Bible is smudged with human fingerprints, then the Psalms may give us the blotchiest pages of all. They are, in the words of British Benedictine Sebastian Moore, "rough-hewn from earthy experience."[10]

"The Psalms don't theologize or explain anger away," wrote author and poet Kathleen Norris, who studied the Psalter as a Benedictine oblate. "One reason for this is that the Psalms are poetry, and poetry's function is not to explain but to offer images and stories that resonate with our lives. . . . In expressing all the complexities and contradictions of human experience, the Psalms act as good psychologists. They defeat our tendency to try to be holy without being human first."[11]

A Benedictine community sings the Psalms at morning, noon, and evening prayers, cycling through the entire Psalter every month. The repetition creates a special intimacy with these ancient words, the images they conjure and emotions they evoke gaining fresh relevance in the changing seasons of both individual and communal life. In the Psalms, you will find the right words for nearly every occasion—anger over an election that turned out all wrong, grief for the loss of a friend, awe at the sight of a sky thick with stars, joy upon entering a sanctuary swelling with worship music.

The Psalms, Norris explained, "demand that we recognize that praise does not spring from a delusion that things are better than they are, but rather from the human capacity for joy."[12]

But the church does not always embrace the messy, unresolved psalms. One study examined the prayer books and hymnals of several prominent Christian denominations to find that the majority of psalms omitted from liturgical use are the laments. Another estimated that while lament constitutes 40 percent of all psalms, it makes up only 13 percent of the hymnal for the Churches of Christ, 19 percent of the Presbyterian hymnal, and 13 percent of the Baptist hymnal.[13] Christian Copyright Licensing International lists the top one hundred worship songs used in contemporary worship each year, and usually only four or five qualify as songs of mourning or frustration.

In his marvelous book *Prophetic Lament,* Soong-Chan Rah explained that lament challenges the status quo by crying out for justice. It runs counter to our American hubris, which focuses on trumpeting our successes. He explained, "The absence of lament in the liturgy of the American church results in a loss of memory. We forget the necessity of lamenting over suffering and pain. We forget the reality of suffering and pain."[14]

We forget, too, that the source of much of that pain is systemic, that many of our brothers and sisters labor beneath the weight of inequality and discrimination. Without lament, Rah wrote, "Any theological reflection that emerges from the suffering 'have-nots' can be minimized in the onslaught of the triumphalism of the 'haves.'"[15]

Often I hear from readers who left their churches because they had no songs for them to sing after the miscarriage, the shooting, the earthquake, the divorce, the diagnosis, the attack, the bankruptcy. That American tendency toward triumphalism, of optimism rooted in success, money, and privilege, will infect and sap of substance any faith community that has lost its capacity for "holding space" for those in grief. As therapists and caregivers explain, to "hold space" for someone is to simply sit with them in their pain, without judgment or solutions, and remain present and attentive no matter the outcome.[16] The Psalms are, in a sense, God's way of holding space for us. They invite us to rejoice, wrestle, cry, complain, offer thanks, and shout obscenities before our Maker without self-consciousness and without fear. Life is full of the sort of joys and sorrows that don't resolve neatly in a major key. God knows that. The Bible knows that. Why don't we?

It is telling, and extraordinary, that in his most vulnerable moment, Jesus himself turned to the Psalms. Hanging from a Roman cross between two thieves, while his mother and loved ones watched in shock, he cried, *"Eli, Eli lema sabachthani?"*

"My God, my God, why have you forsaken me?" (Matthew 27:46).

It's a cry straight from Psalm 22, the God to whom these words were first spoken, speaking them back in human form. Three days later, Jesus would rise from the dead, but in that moment, when all hope was lost and the darkness overwhelmed, only poetry would do.

THE BEAST

They say the beast was driven out of heaven,
And like a leopard, prowls the earth for prey.
It has four heads, though some claim sight of seven.
It wears ten crowns engraved with blasphemy.
What creature past or present can compare
To one who boasts the teeth of lion kings,
But with the mighty haunches of a bear
Leaps, lupine, to soar on eagle's wings?
No legion made of men can it beset,
So nations war and strive to win its favor.
Every Caesar wants it for a pet,
Every superpower for a savior.
All, save the sons and daughters of Abraham,
Who into its carnassial grin send a Lamb.

5

RESISTANCE STORIES

On a muggy June morning in South Carolina, a young black woman named Bree Newsome scaled the thirty-foot flagpole outside the state's capitol building and removed its Confederate flag. As police and protestors shouted at her from the ground, Newsome, just thirty years old and wearing a helmet and harness, shouted back, "In the name of Jesus, this flag has to come down. You come against me with hatred and oppression and violence. I come against you in the name of God. This flag comes down today."[1]

Ten days earlier, white supremacist Dylann Roof had walked into a prayer service at Emanuel African Methodist Episcopal Church in Charleston and after sitting among the congregants for nearly an hour, pulled a handgun from his bag. Aiming first at eighty-seven-year-old Susie Jackson, he killed nine people, including the church's pastor. In pictures on his website, Roof posed with symbols of white supremacy and neo-Nazism, including the Confederate flag, so the massacre had reopened a debate among lawmakers about removing the flag from statehouse grounds.

But as the conversation droned on, and some white citizens pushed back against the potential change, Newsome's spirit grew restless. That flag had flown over the state when her fourth great-grandparents were enslaved there. It had been reraised over the state house in 1962 in defiance of the civil rights movement. Those white stars and blue bars had appeared at countless Ku Klux Klan rallies and lynchings over the decades before they made it to the back of Dylann Roof's Hyundai Elantra as a vanity plate.

That flag was more than just a flag.

"I couldn't sleep," Newsome later recalled. "I sat awake in the dead of night. All the ghosts of the past seemed to be rising."[2]

Unwilling to wait through yet another round of bureaucracy, Newsome collaborated with other activists to formulate a plan of protest designed for maximum visual impact. With the help of her friend James Tyson, a white man who ran support from the ground, Newsome scaled the flagpole on a Saturday morning when protestors were just beginning to gather. She reached the top of the pole as the morning sun bathed the statehouse in light, and the resulting photo—of Newsome clinging to the flagpole, her right arm extended with the dislocated Confederate flag in her fist—went viral. When Newsome reached the ground, she and her friend were arrested. As she was handcuffed, she quoted the Psalms: "The LORD is my light and my salvation, whom shall I fear?" (27:1).

Newsome and Tyson were charged with defacing a monument, but by the time they posted bond, their protest had inspired a movement. The act of civil disobedience put pressure on state officials to remove the flag permanently, which happened, at last, on July 10, 2015—150 years after the Confederacy lost the Civil War.

On a muggy June morning in South Carolina, a young black woman named Bree Newsome scaled the thirty-foot flagpole outside the state's capitol building, looked straight into the eyes of the Beast, and said, "Not today."

༖

The Bible teems with monsters. From the sea dragon Leviathan, with its fearful scales and claws, to the rumbling Behemoth with brasslike bones and cedar-strong tail, to the mysterious giant fish of the Mediterranean Sea that swallowed Jonah whole, the creatures of our holy text practically roar and fulminate from the page. In a vision, Daniel encountered four great beasts—one like a lion with eagle's wings, one like a bear with three ribs in its mouth, another like a leopard with four wings and four heads, and a fourth with iron teeth, bronze claws, and ten horns (Daniel 7). The book of Revelation combines these images into a description of a single monster rising from the sea, resembling a leopard, lion, and bear, with "seven heads and ten horns, and upon his horns ten crowns" (Revelation 13:1 KJV). The beast is joined by a fearsome consort, a fiery-red dragon, whose tail thrashes so widely it sweeps a third of the stars from the sky.

Biblical beasts can represent several things—the awe-inspiring mystery of the natural world, the fearful chaos of the unknown, the sovereignty of God over even the most powerful forces in the universe—but in the case of the mutant creatures of Daniel and Revelation, they represent the evils of oppressive empires.

It's easy for modern-day readers to forget that the Bible was written by oppressed religious minorities living under the heels of powerful nation-states known for their extravagant wealth and violence. For the authors of the Old Testament, it was the Egyptian, Assyrian, Babylonian, Greek, and Persian Empires. For the authors of the New Testament, it was, of course, the massive Roman Empire.

These various superpowers, which inflicted centuries of suffering upon the Jews and other conquered populations, became collectively known among the people of God as *Babylon*.

One of the most important questions facing the people who gave us the Bible was: *How do we resist Babylon, both as an exterior force that opposes the ways of God and an interior pull that tempts us with imitation and assimilation?* They answered with volumes of stories, poems, prophecies, and admonitions grappling with their identity as an exiled people, their anger at the forces that scattered and oppressed them, God's role in their exile and deliverance, and the ultimate hope that one day "Babylon, the jewel of kingdoms, the pride and glory of the Babylonians, will be overthrown by God" (Isaiah 13:19).

It is in this sense that much of Scripture qualifies as resistance literature. It defies the empire by subverting the notion that history will be written by the wealthy, powerful, and cruel, insisting instead that the God of the oppressed will have the final word.

As Pastor Rob Bell observed, "This is what we read, again and again in the pages of the Bible—fearless, pointed, courageous, subversive, poetic, sometimes sarcastic, other times angry, heartfelt, razor-sharp critique of people, nations, systems, and empires endlessly accumulating more at the expense of everybody they're stepping on along the way."[3]

The Bible's resistance stories include heartbreaking poems of lamentation and defiant songs of hope. They give us moments of stinging satire and moments of devastating self-criticism. There are tales of resilience and cleverness in which our heroes navigate everything from a lion's den to a beauty contest to a hostile Assyrian city, and there are highly symbolic visions of a future in which a valley of bones reanimates into an army and a seven-headed beast gets cast into a lake of fire. Resistance stories appear in various forms throughout the Bible, from Genesis to Revelation, sometimes overtly and sometimes with a subtlety that might be missed by the untrained eye. (Remember how the creation narrative of Genesis 1 is meant to stand in contrast to those Babylonian tales of warring gods and goddesses?) While themes of resistance are perhaps most concentrated in the lives and writings of the prophets, they appear anywhere in Scripture that, as Walter Brueggemann put it, "the mythic claims of the empire are ended by the disclosure of the alternate religion of the freedom of God"[4]—which is to say, everywhere.

Perhaps the most significant character in any story of resistance is the prophet. Biblically speaking, a prophet isn't a fortune-teller or soothsayer who predicts the future, but rather a truth-teller who sees things as they really are—past, present, and future—and who challenges their community to both accept that reality and imagine a better one.

"It is the vocation of the prophet to keep alive the ministry of imagination," wrote Brueggemann in his landmark book, *The Prophetic Imagination,* "to keep on conjuring and proposing futures alternative to the single one the king wants to urge as the only thinkable one."[5]

This calling gives us some of Scripture's most memorable characters. Jeremiah, for example, wore an ox yoke around his neck to symbolize Israel's impending oppression under the Babylonian Empire. Ezekiel memorialized the fall of Jerusalem by building a model of the city and lying down next to it for over a year—390 days on his left side and 40 days on his right side—eating only bread cooked over cow dung at meals. When a group of teenage boys taunted the prophet Elisha's baldness, God sent two female bears to maul them to death. (My youth pastor liked to tease his students with that story when we commented on his receding hairline.) When Jonah tried to avoid God's call to preach in the dangerous Assyrian city of Nineveh,

God sent a giant fish to swallow the prophet up for three days before spitting him out on the closest shoreline. Hosea married a prostitute to make a point. John the Baptist famously took to the wilderness, subsisting on locusts and honey and urging the people to "repent, for the kingdom of heaven has come near" (Matthew 3:2).

In other words, the prophets are weirdos. More than anyone else in Scripture, they remind us that those odd ducks shouting from the margins of society may see things more clearly than the political and religious leaders with the inside track. We ignore them at our own peril.

The prophets, explained Brueggemann, "are moved the way every good poet is moved to have to describe the world differently according to the gifts of their insight. And, of course, in their own time and every time since, the people that control the power structure do not know what to make of them, so they characteristically try to silence them. What power people always discover is that you cannot finally silence poets."[6]

Before the Babylonian exile, prophets like Samuel, Nathan, Elijah, Elisha, and Huldah spoke out against the abuses of Israel's priesthood and monarchy, warning that if the nation continued to indulge in immorality, idolatry, and injustice, God would hand the people over to their enemies. Sometimes the rulers listened to the prophets. King David famously repented after the prophet Nathan rebuked him for murdering Bathsheba's husband, and King Josiah yielded to the prophetess Huldah's authentication and interpretation of previously neglected Scripture. But most of the time, speaking truth to power put the prophets on the wrong side of the law. King Ahab called Elijah "you troubler of Israel" for speaking out against injustice and banished the prophet to the wilderness, where Elijah relied on ravens to bring him bread (1 Kings 18:17). Queen Jezebel sent hundreds of prophets into hiding for challenging her insatiable greed (though the prophets got the last word on that one, as Jezebel was eventually thrown from a window and eaten by dogs). John the Baptist was beheaded by Herod Antipas, not for following Jesus, but for criticizing the noble family's excess and lechery.

The prophets directed their most stinging critiques at the leaders of their own community. The violence and excess of the empire was a given, but when Israel itself indulged in greed and sexual exploitation, when it oppressed its workers and neglected the poor, the prophets got really angry. The prophet Ezekiel compared Israel's sins to those of the wicked cities of Sodom and Gomorrah, noting, "Now this was the sin of your sister Sodom: She and her daughters were arrogant, overfed and unconcerned; they did not help the poor and needy" (Ezekiel 16:49).

Even the religious elites were not exempt from prophetic critique. The prophet Amos was so enraged that Israel carried on with empty worship practices while exploiting the poor and oppressed, he channeled the wrath of God, declaring:

> I hate, I despise your religious festivals;
>> your assemblies are a stench to me.
> Even though you bring me burnt offerings and grain offerings,
>> I will not accept them. . . .
> Away with the noise of your songs!
>> I will not listen to the music of your harps.
> But let justice roll on like a river,
>> righteousness like a never-failing stream!
>
> (AMOS 5:21–24)

Once the monarchy was destroyed and Jerusalem sacked, the prophets took on the role of public lamenters, filling pages and pages of Scripture with songs of mourning.

Some of the most vivid images come from Jeremiah, who sang, "Oh that my head were waters, and my eyes a fountain of tears, that I might weep day and night for the slain daughter of my people!" (Jeremiah 9:1 ESV). Jeremiah's particular skill at lament often lends him the moniker "prophet of doom," though this articulation of the reality of suffering is a crucial part of both truth-telling and healthy grief.

Alongside these cries of anguish and anger, condemnation and critique, the prophets deliver what is perhaps the most subversive element of any resistance movement: *hope.* Employing language and imagery charged with theological meaning, the prophet asserted, despite all evidence to the contrary, that the God of Israel—the God of slaves and exiles and despised religious minorities—remains present and powerful, enthroned over all creation and above every empire.

In the book of Isaiah, an anonymous prophet, sometimes referred to as Second Isaiah, described in luscious detail the enthronement festival of the one true God.

> See, the Sovereign LORD comes with power,
>> and he rules with a mighty arm. . . .
> He tends his flock like a shepherd:
>> He gathers the lambs in his arms
> and carries them close to his heart.
>
> (ISAIAH 40:10–11)

"Take comfort, my people," the prophet essentially cried again and again, "I have good news and joyous tidings! Our God reigns, now and forever."

Second Isaiah even went so far as to mock the gods of Babylon whose images must be carried around on the backs of cattle, their weight a burden on man and beast alike. The poet-prophet contrasted this with Yahweh, depicted in Isaiah 46 as a mother carrying the descendants of Jacob in her womb, speaking tenderly to them, as if in a lullaby, "I have made you and I will carry you; I will sustain you and I will rescue you" (v. 4).

The book of Isaiah rings with some of the most beautiful poetry the Bible offers us. Even the most cynical reader can't help but soften at the image of a God who gathers his sheep in his arms like a shepherd, who carried her children in her womb like a mother, who will "swallow up death forever" and "wipe away the tears from all faces" (25:8). Is it any wonder the words of Isaiah appear so often in the preaching of John the Baptist and Martin Luther King Jr.? That sort of language has staying power.

In addition to the prophets, resistance literature recounts the stories of unlikely political dissidents, like Daniel, a noble Jew who masterfully negotiates life in the courts of King Nebuchadnezzar of Babylon, keeping God's law amid temptation, calling pagan rulers to account, and surviving a night in a lions' den after his political rivals grow jealous. When Daniel's friends, Shadrach, Meshach, and Abednego, refuse to bow to Nebuchadnezzar's golden statue during a state parade, they are thrown into a fiery furnace, where all three survive without a single singe. The books of Ezra, Nehemiah, and Esther recount the tenuous relationship between the Jews and the Persian Empire, which ranges from the empire's support for rebuilding Jerusalem's walls to a storied attempt at genocide (more on that story, and Queen Esther, later).

Throughout the Bible's resistance stories, we encounter examples of apocalyptic literature. The word *apocalypse* means "unveiling" or "disclosing." An apocalyptic event or vision, therefore, reveals things as they really are. It peels back the layers of pomp and pretense, fear and uncertainty, to expose the true forces at work in the world. Using highly symbolic, theologically charged language, the authors of Scripture employ apocalyptic literature to dramatize the work of the Resistance, to offer hope to those suffering under the weight of an empire that seems, on the surface, all-powerful and unassailable.

So when the prophets Daniel and John envision the empires as vicious beasts, what they're saying is, *Beneath all the wealth, power, and excess of these dazzling empires lie grotesque monsters, trampling everyone and everything in their path.* And when they depict God as tolerating, then restraining, and finally destroying these monsters, what they're saying is, *The story isn't over; even the greatest empires are no match for goodness, righteousness, and justice.*

It might not look like it now, but the Resistance is winning.

Fairy tales are more than true: not because they tell us that dragons exist, but because they tell us that dragons can be defeated.

The beasts of Daniel and Revelation need not be literal to be real. To the people who first read the Bible, they were as real as the imperial soldiers who marched down their streets, the royal edicts that threatened their homes and livelihoods, and the heavy fear that crept into every fitful dream, every visit to the market, every hushed conversation about what to do if the emperor demanded their worship or their death.

"The point of apocalyptic texts is not to predict the future," explained biblical scholar Amy-Jill Levine in *The Meaning of the Bible*; "it is to provide comfort in the present. The Bible is not a book of teasers in which God has buried secrets only to be revealed three millennia later." Rather, she argued, apocalyptic texts "proclaim that a guiding hand controls history, and assure that justice will be done."[7]

But a lot of Christians, especially American Christians, prefer instead, wild, futuristic stories about children vanishing out of their clothes, airplanes dropping from the sky, pestilence overtaking the earth, and a Democrat getting elected president—the stuff of paperbacks and Christian B movies. And I think that's because Americans, particularly white Americans, have a hard time catching apocalyptic visions when they benefit too much from the status quo to want a peek behind the curtain. When you belong to the privileged class of the most powerful global military superpower in the world, it can be hard to relate to the oppressed minorities who wrote so much of the Bible. (And no, their oppression did not consist of getting wished "Happy Holidays" instead of "Merry Christmas" at Target. That's not actual persecution, folks.) The fact is, the shadow under which most of the world trembles today belongs to America, and its beasts could be named any number of things— White Supremacy, Colonialism, the Prison Industrial Complex, the War Machine, Civil Religion, Materialism, Greed.

Now, lest you think I'm an America-hater who can't see the value in good citizenship, you should know I served proudly on an advisory council to the White House for a time, lobbied that "Stars and Stripes Forever" be played as the recessional at my wedding ceremony (though that idea was overruled by less-patriotic participants), and can remember with precision the entirety of my sixth-grade choreographed routine to Lee Greenwood's "Proud to Be an American." (You remember yours too; admit it.) I've done enough international travel to understand that American citizenship comes with immense benefit, and I love this country for its diversity, ingenuity, and high aspirations.

America's no ancient Babylon or Rome, I know that. But America's no kingdom of God either.

If you doubt it, study an old diagram of a slave ship. Try to count the number of chained-up bodies drawn flatly in the cargo hold, and multiply that by hundreds of thousands, representing the nearly half a million Africans brought to America in the slave trade. Then remember that each of those bodies represents the very real life of a very real human being, created in the image of God, with memories and ideas and quirks and fears, and that those who survived the voyage across the Middle Passage were brutally enslaved by people who claimed to be Christians.

Or consider the Trail of Tears, and try to imagine what it would be like to be a Cherokee mother, driven out of your home by the US government, stripped of your belongings, and forced to walk thousands of miles with your small children, from Georgia to Oklahoma, without enough food or medical care—all because white men wanted the gold on your land. More than four thousand Cherokees, including many mothers and children, died from exposure, disease, and starvation while making that gruesome march. Imagine watching your toddler die of hunger in the snow.

Or google the history of child labor in the United States, or its treatment of the mentally ill in so-called "lunatic asylums," or Japanese internment during World War II, or Jim Crow, or the nine hundred Jewish refugees aboard the *St. Louis* who were turned away from the United States and sent back to Europe to face the Holocaust. Or find out if the children of Flint, Michigan, have access to clean water yet.

The fact is, despite wistful nostalgia for the days when America was a supposedly "Christian nation," the history of this country is littered with the bodies of innocent men, women, and children who were neglected, enslaved, dispossessed, and slaughtered so the privileged class could have more and more and more and more.

More land.
More money.
More power.
More status.

More furs, more guns, more profits, more amenities, more
square footage, more security, more fame.

And these are not just ghosts of the past. Having been histor-
ically dispossessed and discriminated against, African American
and indigenous communities continue to face higher rates of poverty and crime, and struggle disproportionately for access to quality
education, healthy food, secure housing, and affordable health care.
The United States has the highest incarceration rate in the world;
and even though roughly the same number of white people use
drugs as African Americans, African Americans are sent to prison
for drug offenses at six times the rate of whites.[8] While the ultrarich
get richer, middle- and lower-income wages have stagnated so that
the number of "working poor" in America continues to grow. In
many states, you can still get fired from your job for simply being
gay, but you can be a serial womanizer who brags about grabbing
married women "by the pussy" and still get elected president.

There's just no denying that the very things for which Israel
was condemned by the prophets—gross income inequality, mistreatment of immigrants and refugees, carelessness toward life, the
oppression of the poor and vulnerable, and the worship of money,
sex, and violence—remain potent, prevalent sins in our culture.
These sins are embedded in nearly every system of our society from
education to law enforcement to entertainment to religion. We are
all culpable, all responsible for working for change.

Yet rather than confessing our sins, and rather than disman-
tling the systems that perpetuate them, many Christians shrug it off
as part of an irrelevant past or spin out religious-sounding rhetoric
about peace and reconciliation without engaging in the hard work
of repentance and restitution. Ever the quick-fix culture, we want
oppressed people to "just get over it," to move on and let the injustice

go. I've heard many black preachers liken the church's response to racism in America to the words of Jeremiah, who cried, "They dress the wound of my people as though it were not serious. 'Peace, peace,' they say, when there is no peace" (Jeremiah 6:14).

Saying we are a nation of peace doesn't make it so—not for Trayvon Martin, not for Tamir Rice, not for the twenty kindergartners shot at Sandy Hook Elementary School, not for that Cherokee mama, not for the Iraqi villagers in the crosshairs of our drones. Tensions around issues of injustice must not be avoided in the name of an easy peace and cheap grace, but rather passionately engaged, until justice rolls down like a river, righteousness like a never-failing stream.

My friend Jonathan Martin, who is a third-generation Pentecostal preacher, described the election of Donald Trump as an apocalyptic event—not in the sense that it brought on the end of the world, but in the sense that it uncovered, or revealed, divides and contours in the American social landscape many of us did not want to face, deep rifts regarding race, religion, nationalism, gender, and fear. It was certainly apocalyptic for me in the way that it exposed, to my shame, my reluctance to resist certain injustices in this country until the resistance movement fit more conveniently with my political persuasions.

For too long, the white American church has chosen the promise of power over prophetic voice. We have allied ourselves with the empire and, rather than singing songs of hopeful defiance with the exiles, created more of them. We have, consciously and unconsciously, done the bidding of the Beast—not in every case, of course, but in far too many.

This is why it's so important to follow the lead of modern-day prophets like Bree Newsome who, in scaling that flagpole, removing the Confederate flag, and declaring God's reign over and above the centuries-long reign of white supremacy, honored a long and storied tradition of prophetic protest. Her actions helped my generation visualize a better future. She simultaneously revealed things as they are and how they might be.

We must listen too to Rev. William Barber of North Carolina, who, though he struggles with a severe arthritic spinal condition and bursitis in his left knee, has marched and preached for decades on civil rights, pressing upon elected leaders and private citizens alike the moral imperative to "shock this nation with the power of love."[8]

I think also of my clergywomen friends, who, in the face of near-constant obstruction and all kinds of sexist double standards, preach the Word, run soup kitchens, anoint the sick, tend to the dying, sponsor refugees, get arrested at protests, and speak truth to power, day in and day out, with little thanks or praise. I think of Jeremy Courtney of the Preemptive Love Coalition, whose work providing medical care for families in Iraq led him to advocate tirelessly on behalf of refugees and to challenge the complicity of American Christians in turning those refugees away.

And then there are the many prophets outside the United States, like the Coptic Christians of Egypt who, after terrorists bombed two churches on Palm Sunday 2017, showed up to church in unprecedented numbers seven days later to celebrate the risen Christ, their numbers literally spilling out the doors and onto the streets. Sometimes just showing up to the communion table is a way of looking straight into the eyes of the Beast and saying, "Not today."

These are the people telling today's resistance stories, drawing from the Bible's deep well of prophetic examples for inspiration and strength. Though political, they avoid partisanship; though clear-eyed, they remain stubbornly hopeful. The prophet's voice is routinely dismissed as too critical (or too "bitter" if she happens to be a woman), but she always challenges from a place of deep love for her community.

What I love about the Bible is that the story isn't over. There are still prophets in our midst. There are still dragons and beasts. It might not look like it, but the Resistance is winning. The light is breaking through.

So listen to the weirdos. Listen to the voices crying from the wilderness. They are pointing us to a new King and a better kingdom.

As Jesus said, "Let those with ears, hear."

⌁

A teenage boy wearing a black cape and felt hat strolls across the stage. Behind him, a cavalcade of middle school princesses, pirates, and superheroes bows.

"Make way for Lord Haman!" cries the caller, a boy of eleven or twelve wearing a Mad Hatter costume.

At Haman's name, the audience erupts into a deafening roar, drowning the villain's words in boos, catcalls, and thunderous stomps. From the back, a drunken woman screams, "Go away!" and the room ripples with giggles.

Onstage, only Mordecai stands erect, declaring with muffled defiance through his costume beard, "I only bow to God!"

The audience cheers.

"What kind of man is this?" asks Haman of a nearby Princess Elsa.

"A Jew," she replies.

Everyone in the audience knows what's next . . .

It's a strange way to mark a thwarted genocide, but every year, this is how Jews across the world celebrate Purim, a holiday recounting the tale of Haman, Mordecai, King Xerxes, and Queen Esther—one of the best resistance stories in Scripture.

As Lauren Winner wrote,

> Purim is like Halloween and Mardi Gras and bunch of other stuff all mixed up together. It's a holiday in which there's revelry and inversion and people all dress up. They wear masks. When you go to the synagogue to hear the book of Esther read, you are instructed by the rabbis to shout and scream whenever you hear the name Haman so that his name gets drowned out. You're also instructed to get really drunk on Purim, so drunk, the rabbis say, that you can no longer tell the difference between Haman's name and the king's name.[9]

Indeed, the biblical story, which tells how Mordecai and Esther helped saved their people from a pogrom by the Persian Empire, lends itself to such an interpretation. Many of the characters, particularly those of the Persian court, are so hapless and exaggerated, you can't help but laugh. Nearly every major plot point unfolds at some banquet, and the text includes all sorts of dramatic twists and turns. It's a story fit for the stage.

Yet the text itself includes some disturbing details. As a kid, I always imagined Queen Esther to be something of a beauty pageant contestant. Having received the PG version of the tale in church, I figured that in addition to the "twelve months of beautification" Esther underwent before meeting King Xerxes, she must have performed some kind of talent and answered questions from a glass bowl before winning the heart of a love-struck royal. I never learned in Sunday school that Esther, whose Jewish name was Hadassah, was forced, along with perhaps thousands of virgin girls from Susa, into King Xerxes's harem. Or that the king had banished his first wife, Queen Vashti, for refusing to publicly flaunt her body before his drunken friends. Or that under the care of the royal eunuchs, Esther and the women of the king's harem each took a turn in the king's bed to see who would please him best. Or that the women received just one night with the king, after which they were transferred to the eunuchs in charge of the concubines, with the instruction not to return to the king's chamber unless summoned by name, under the penalty of death.

They left those details out of the flannelgraphs.

The book of Esther is grouped with the Ketuvim or "Writings," of Hebrew Scripture, and is set during a time of historical transition. In 539 BC, Cyrus came to the throne of the Persian Empire and defeated the Babylonians. Cyrus allowed some of the Jews to return to Jerusalem to rebuild the temple, while others remained displaced. The events unfold in the formidable capital of the Persian Empire during the reign of King Xerxes, an arrogant Eastern despot who exercised complete control over the many people who found themselves swept up in his vast empire.

The Greek historian Herodotus, author of *History of the Persian Wars*, wrote just twenty-five years after the reign of Xerxes and provided some insight into his might and cruelty, including the fact that five hundred young boys were gathered each year from the kingdom and castrated to serve as eunuchs in the Persian court.[10] It's important to remember that the bodies of these eunuchs, and the bodies of the women like Esther who were forced into the royal harem, were the property of the empire. This was the forced concubinage of women who, in a patriarchal culture in an occupied territory, had no authority over their own marriages or bodies.

The story begins with a banquet. At the height of his glory and wealth, King Xerxes throws a lavish, multiday celebration for all the nobles of his court. He hosts feasts day and night in the palace garden, where fine linens hang from marble pillars and merrymakers lounge on couches made of gold. The king tells his servants to give each man as much wine as he wants to drink, so as the days wear on, the party grows wilder.

On the seventh day, when Xerxes is "in high spirits from wine," he commands his eunuchs to bring Queen Vashti to the garden. He wants to display his wife's body before all the drunken men of the court, for she is "lovely to look at" (Esther 1:10–11).

Well, when the attendants deliver the king's command, Vashti refuses to obey. The woman simply won't come out.

Her defiance infuriates the king, who consults his closest advisers on how to respond to his wife's disobedience. A confidant named Memukan takes advantage and turns this little domestic dispute into a full-blown national crisis.

"The queen's conduct will become known to all the women," he warns, "and so they will despise their husbands and say, 'King Xerxes commanded Queen Vashti to be brought before him, but she would not come.' This very day the Persian and Median women of the nobility who have heard about the queen's conduct will respond to all the king's nobles in the same way. There will be no end of disrespect and discord" (Esther 1:17–18).

At Memukan's suggestion, Xerxes issues a royal decree to be written into the laws of Persia and Media, that Vashti will never again enter the presence of the king and that the king will bestow her royal position on someone else, someone who is "better than she" (v. 19). The decree, delivered to every province and in every language of the empire, proclaims that "all the women will respect their husbands, from the least to the greatest" and that "every man should be ruler of his own household" (vv. 20, 22).

The overreaction is downright comical.

Audiences at Purim plays roar with laughter at these pathetic, insecure men, so threatened by one woman's autonomy that they issue kingdom-wide edicts declaring men the rulers of their homes.

133

But behind the joke is a warning. Xerxes and his court have a habit of making major, national decisions based on personal offense and whims. Beneath the pomp and wealth is a dangerous fragility with which our heroes, and the Jewish people, must contend.

After banishing Vashti, the king gets lonely. Once his "fury had subsided" (2:1), he is persuaded by his attendants to search the land for its most beautiful virgins with the goal of finding a new, more obedient queen. Among the women forced into the harem is Esther, a beautiful Jewish orphan under the care of her cousin, Mordecai. While preparing for her encounter with the king, Esther wins the favor of everyone she meets, including the royal eunuchs, who, like Esther, had themselves been taken and used by the king. The cunning eunuchs pull more strings in the palace than anyone realizes, and they prove important allies as the story unfolds.

With the help of the eunuchs, Esther is chosen queen, though she is forbidden from speaking with the king without a summons. No one in the palace knows she is a Jew. Meanwhile, Mordecai, too, is commended when he uncovers an assassination plot by two of King Xerxes's courtiers. The cousins seem poised to live a relatively privileged lifestyle among the occupying empire, until Haman—*Booooooo!*—is appointed viceroy.

When Mordecai refuses to bow to Haman as he passes, Haman's fury turns to disdain for all Jews. The villain convinces a disinterested, persuadable King Xerxes to exterminate every Jew in the empire, then sends dispatches throughout the land with the order to "destroy, kill, and annihilate all the Jews—young and old, women and children—on a single day" (3:13). Haman chooses the day by casting lots, the fate of an entire race left to a game of chance. (The word *pur* is Persian for "lot"; thus, the holiday is known as Purim.) While the Jews fast and pray in fear, King Xerxes and Haman celebrate over drinks. The text says, "The city of Susa was bewildered" (v. 15).

Terrified for his people, Mordecai implores Esther to intercede with the king, urging that perhaps she has "come to royal position for such a time as this" (4:14). After three days of fasting, Esther works up the courage to approach the throne without a summons. To her relief, the king extends his scepter to indicate her life will be spared. Esther invites both the king and Haman to a series of banquets, setting just the right stage to reveal her true identity.

Meanwhile, Haman plots to have Mordecai hanged, but a bout with insomnia leads King Xerxes to a bunch of old court records that remind him that Mordecai has yet to be honored for saving his life. (King Xerxes, you will find, is a rather forgetful fellow.) In a deliciously ironic scene, King Xerxes asks Haman how a man faithful to the king ought to be honored. Assuming Xerxes is referring to Haman himself, he tells the king to throw a grand parade for the man, dress him in the king's royal robes and give him a royal horse, and declare throughout the city that this is how a man who loves his king will be praised. Imagine Haman's horror when King Xerxes tells him to do these things for Mordecai!

Mordecai gets his parade, Haman goes home to cry to his wife, and Esther plans her big reveal.

At Esther's second banquet, she tells the king that her people have been targeted for genocide and begs him for mercy. The king is horrified. "Who on earth would plan such a thing?" he essentially demands, his previous conversation with Haman about eliminating an entire people group apparently slipping his mind.

Esther points to the villain. "An adversary and enemy! This vile Haman!"

Haman, seeing he's been bested, falls onto Esther's couch in agony to beg for pardon. Xerxes interprets this as the man making a pass at his wife, and Haman's fate is sealed. The villain is hanged on the very gallows he had prepared for Mordecai. Esther secures permission for the Jews to take revenge on their enemies, on the very day those enemies had planned to eliminate them. The story ends in a Tarantino-style bloodbath.

Many people notice that the book of Esther is the only one in Scripture that fails to mention God, and indeed its religious themes are covert. However, God's presence is discernible, not simply in the providential unfolding of the Jewish people's deliverance, but as a contrast to the impotent, aimless reign of the bumbling King Xerxes and his Persian court. Though intent on flaunting the "vast wealth of his kingdom and the splendor of his majesty" (1:4), Xerxes turns out to be little more than a pathetic puppet, coaxed and coddled by advisers, eunuchs, and villains, and ultimately controlled by a Jewish orphan and her cousin. Haman's rage against the Jews is petty and childish. Major empire-wide decisions get made, not after prayer and fasting, but over drinks at banquets or by casting lots. The story of Esther pulls back the veil on the empire to reveal that behind the golden chairs and packed harems and patriarchal edicts are a bunch of insecure, weak men whose attempts to puff themselves up only make them look silly. It is an empty, foolish power. The emperor has no clothes.

This would all be terribly frightening were it not for the quiet, and at times hidden, hand of God, working all things together for good. I suspect this is why the Jews dress up in costume, feast, celebrate, and laugh in response to a story about their near destruction as a people. They laugh because, like a thrown-together middle school Purim play, the power of the empire is just a big show. In the end, the God of Israel—of Abraham, Moses, and Esther—gets the last word, using the weak to humble the powerful.

I include the story of Esther as a resistance story because this dramatic tale from exile, and its reenactment each year in the Purim play, sanctify satire as a ready weapon in the arsenal of holy resistance. Sometimes the best way to fell the Beast is to look it in the face and laugh. Beneath the bared teeth and bloodied claws lies a frightened little kitten, insecure about its hair. For a people whose history involves far too many stories like this one, such laughter is subversive. It is comforting as well, for it suggests that while Persia casts the lots, God holds history, and he can outwit even the most unpredictable regimes to deliver and preserve the vulnerable.

I include the story, too, because it's one of my favorites. What sparked my imagination as a little girl stirs my faith today, reminding me that a misogynistic king running a dangerously dysfunctional superpower is nothing new and nothing God can't handle.

Maybe a little biblically inspired dark comedy is just what we need "for such a time as this."

γ_0

"A third of the stars will fall from the sky."

"The sea will give up her dead."

"The Whore of Babylon will ride the Great Beast."

"Only those whose names are written in the Book of Life will live."

Whenever I mention the book of Revelation, my husband, Dan, likes to tease me by snapping into a trancelike recitation of these strange prophecies he memorized as a child. Indeed, Revelation's intense, bizarre imagery makes it perhaps the best known, and least understood, example of apocalyptic resistance literature in the Bible. Even the ancients struggled with how to interpret a story that gives us rivers of blood, a lake of fire, a giant monster with seven heads and ten horns, and a seven-eyed lamb opening seven seals.

It's important to understand that Revelation is not some coded message about the distant future, sent out into the ether to be scrutinized by televangelists centuries later, but rather a letter, written to real people, living at a real time in history, asking very real and pressing questions about their immediate circumstances. Its author, a seer named John, had been exiled to the island of Patmos, where he wrote to challenge and encourage Christians suffering intense persecution under the Roman Empire, probably during the reign of Domitian.

These Christians were inundated with propaganda from the empire. Declarations of the divinity of Caesar, and of the inevitability of his eternal reign, appeared on their coins, at their markets, across the banners waved by occupying soldiers, and in the edicts and laws that threatened their way of life. Domitian even commissioned a choir to follow him everywhere he went, singing, "You are worthy, our lord and god, to receive honor and glory and power." The message from Rome was clear: Submit to the cult of the emperor, and you live. Refuse, and you face censure, imprisonment, or even death.

Convinced things would get worse before they got better, John wrote to both warn and comfort the afflicted. He did this by appealing to their shared theological and literary heritage, making at least 250 references to Hebrew Scripture in a letter that can veer from cryptic prophecy, to pastoral advice, to spontaneous worship in a matter of sentences.

Of particular interest to John, and to many other first-century Jews, was the vision from Daniel 7, which culminates with the Ancient of Days sitting in judgment from a throne of flames, condemning the four fearsome beasts representing Mesopotamia's oppressive empires and transferring their power to "one like a son of man," whose "dominion is an everlasting dominion that will not pass away, and his kingdom is one that will never be destroyed" (Daniel 7:13–14). Gone are the monstrous mutations that only live to destroy. All the nations worship the son of man, or "the human one" in some translations—a king who cries and bleeds and sings and laughs.

There was much speculation in John's day about who this "son of man" might be. The mysterious figure appears in enough prophetic literature for the ancient scribes and rabbis to identify him as the Messiah, or Anointed One. It was expected that the Messiah would rise up among the Jewish people, liberate them from their oppressors, and establish a just, righteous kingdom that, unlike every other empire's, would endure forever.

With every strange, apocalyptic image and every colorful reference to Old Testament prophecy, John was saying one thing loud and clear: Jesus of Nazareth is that person. Jesus of Nazareth is the Messiah, the Son of man, the Lamb who will vanquish the Beast. To Jesus, John said, all the angels and prophets and emperors and people sing a *new* song:

> "Worthy is the Lamb, who was slain,
>> to receive power and wealth and wisdom and strength and
>> honor and glory and praise!"
>
> (REVELATION 5:12)

This was a direct challenge to the empire. No one in John's day would have mistaken it for anything else.

The proclamation of Jesus as king, over and against Caesar, has become such a mainstay of religious parlance we hardly notice we're participating in resistance rhetoric when we say it. Doing or saying something "in the name of Jesus" speaks in defiant contrast to edicts carried out "in the name of Caesar" or "in the name of the king" or "by the authority of the president." Declaring "Jesus is Lord" implies by default that the present rulers are not as sovereign as they seem. Even calling Jesus the Son of God originally stood in specific contrast to the leaders of Rome, who demanded they be known by that very title.

John, and, as we shall see, the rest of the gospel writers, made a bold declaration about the true nature of things that N. T. Wright summed up like this: "God . . . has become king—in and through Jesus! A new state of affairs has been brought into existence. A door has been opened that nobody can shut. Jesus is now the world's rightful Lord, and all other lords are to fall at his feet."[11]

As we move to the stories from the Gospels, it's important to remember that these stories don't begin with "Once upon a time," but with "And it came to pass in those days, that there went out a decree from Caesar Augustus . . ." (Luke 2:1–3 kjv). They are rooted in the context of empire and resistance, of oppression and defiance. To announce the birth of a new royal heir or to celebrate a military victory in a distant land, imperial messengers would issue proclamations of *evangelion*, or "good news." So when Jesus made the following announcement, quoting the prophet Isaiah, the people knew exactly what he meant:

> The Spirit of the Lord is on me,
>> because he has anointed me
>> to proclaim good news to the poor.
> He has sent me to proclaim freedom for the prisoners
>> and recovery of sight for the blind,
>> to set the oppressed free,
>> to proclaim the year of the Lord's favor.
>
> (LUKE 4:18–19)

Jesus takes the Resistance beyond prophecy, beyond songs of hope and lamentation, beyond satire and mockery, and beyond apocalyptic visions to declare the inauguration of a new kingdom. With his birth, teachings, death, and resurrection, Jesus has started a revolution.

It just doesn't look the way anyone expects.

THE WATER

I went to the well at noon.

Sun burning my neck, sweat stinging my eyes, I sighed to think how much heavier that water jar would seem on the journey back. Even the field mice had retreated to the cover of rocks, the sheep to the shade of a lone sycamore.

Most of the women gather at first light, when the dew still clings to the grass and the sun glows soft and pink in the sky, their laughter carrying over the countryside like birdsong as they gossip and banter, chide their toddlers and share news. In the desert, wells give and draw life, their waters evocative of the womb. Wells are where our ancestors arranged marriages, fell in love, and received word of impending births. Wells are where God starts something new.

I was not a woman who belonged at a well.

This spring was named for Jacob, but as I trudged toward it, thirsty, I thought of Tamar, as I often did. Tamar, the original cursed woman, passed from brother to brother, bearing no children, bringing nothing but death, until finally, through lurid means, she gave that family twins and our people a nation. I saw myself in her story, for I too lived in my father-in-law's house, waiting for a little boy to become a man. That boy's mother had every reason to fear me, to hate me. After four weddings and four tragedies, I cannot blame her. Tamar's husbands were wicked, but mine were kind. They honored the law even after superstitious neighbors told them to be done with it, to cast me out into the wilderness to die. The mother, no doubt, wishes they had. Sometimes I did too.

As the sun beat down like a great unseeing eye overhead, I saw a figure seated at the well. A man. I drew closer, spied the knotted tassels on the fringe of his coat confirming he was a Jew, and felt a rush of relief. *Good. We won't have to talk.* A man in this country rarely speaks to a woman. A Jew to a Samaritan? Never.

At last I reached the well, collapsing on the other side to catch my breath. Somewhere a hawk screeched, her eyes, no doubt, on those field mice.

"Will you give me a drink?"

His voice startled me, like a crack of thunder on a clear day. For a moment, I doubted I'd heard it. What sort of Jew asked a Samaritan for water? They believed even our pitchers were unclean.

"You are a Jewish man, and I am a Samaritan woman," I said with a laugh, wary of meeting his eyes. "And you're asking me for water?"

"If you knew who I was," he answered, "you'd be asking *me* for a drink, and I would give you fresh, flowing water, water that is colder and cleaner than this. I would give you the kind of water you really crave."

Now he had my attention. In spite of my exhaustion, I stood to face him. The man was young, maybe thirty. He had no jar, rope, or buckets. He must have been traveling from Judea to Galilee, but I wondered why he journeyed without companions.

"Artesian water from this well?" I pressed. "Sir, you don't even have a bucket to draw with, and this well is deep. Are you saying you are better than our ancestor Jacob, who dug this well and drank from it, along with all his children and livestock? Are you saying you know something he didn't?"

I couldn't help myself. Jews were so smug about religion. No doubt this man never dreamed a Samaritan woman thought of such things.

"Everyone who drinks water from this well will get thirsty again," he said. "But whoever drinks the water I offer will remain satisfied, for they will have a gushing spring inside of them that never runs dry."

"Well then give me some of that water!" I laughed, playing along. "Then I won't have to hike out to this well every day."

The man fell silent. Assuming I'd offended him, I prepared my bucket and lowered it into the well. Of course I planned to give the stranger the first drink. Samaritans, for all you've heard of us, honor the customs of hospitality.

"Go, call your husband and come back," he said, breaking the silence.

My jaw clenched.

"I have no husband," I said.

"Indeed you don't. You've had five husbands, haven't you? And the man you live with now is not one of them."

Five.

This man knew more than what local gossip could carry. He knew my secret. He knew *me.*

Shaking, I let the rope slip. My bucket plunged into the water, and I staggered backward.

"I see you are a prophet," I said, sitting down.

The man said nothing in reply, so for a while we just sat there together under the sun, sweating and thirsty, a strange understanding growing between us. He went to the well and pulled the bucket up.

"So tell me something," I said, recovering my courage.

"Samaritans say the place of rightful worship is that mountain over there, but Jews say it is in Jerusalem. Who is right?"

It may seem like a strange thing to ask a prophet who has just laid your life bare, naming the thing you never dared voice out loud, but if God was speaking to me through a Jew, I had some questions. The enmity between our people stretched back centuries. Though we shared a common ancestry—the same fathers of the faith, the same prophets and kings of old—time and geography had given us different cultures, different practices, different sacred places. The Jews destroyed our temple on Mount Gerizim a hundred years before I was born, then banned us from worshiping in Jerusalem after some of our people desecrated their temple with corpses. If this man was a prophet, it meant righteousness belonged to the Jews. And if righteousness belonged to the Jews, a woman like me had no place to meet with God.

"Don't worry about that," he answered, a smile in his voice. "Salvation will come through the Jews, yes, but it will be for all people. The day is coming when all the barriers between us will collapse. God is Spirit, after all, and Truth. You can't build a temple around Spirit. You can't lock Truth in a shrine. The kind of worship God wants is the kind of worship without walls."

He paused.

"But you know that already, daughter, don't you? You have known all along."

He crouched down and looked me straight in the eyes, seeing me in a way no man had ever seen me before.

"They say a Messiah will come and make all these things plain," I ventured from the ground.

"I—the one speaking to you—am he."

At that, he handed me the bucket of water. I brought it to my lips, lifted my head, and drank deep of the coolest, richest water I ever tasted. I drank and drank and drank. I drank until I could no longer breathe.

When I finished, I wiped my mouth on my sleeve and handed the bucket back to the man, who, to my amazement, threw his head back and gulped the rest of it down, dousing his dusty face with the last splash that remained. For a moment, I doubted what I'd just witnessed. This man, this Jew—this *Messiah*—drank from my defiled cup. And with relish.

He saw my surprise and laughed, the deep belly laugh of a man who sees our religious absurdities for what they are. I joined him, all the tired and thirsty cells in my body awake with life once again. It was like giving birth and being born at the same time.

We laughed and dried our faces until we realized a crowd had gathered. At least ten men, all of them Jews, stood around us, faces stricken.

The man, whom they called Teacher, assured his friends that no laws had been broken, then told the men to prepare for a longer stay.

"We'll be feasting with Samaritans tonight," he declared.

I'm certain that in spite of myself, I beamed.

I had to tell someone, but who? My household hated me. My friends were uneducated peasants with little influence over public affairs. Would anyone believe me? Could anyone understand?

There was Miriam, of course, the slave. And Mara, the prostitute. The baker always liked a good story, and maybe those shepherd boys would too.

As more names and faces came to my mind, my feet moved faster. I ran over the hillside and past the sycamore.

The widow next door could host a banquet. The blind beggar from the alley would certainly come. Perhaps the lepers of Ebal would join us for supper, and maybe a tax collector or two.

My feet pounded the ground as the town came into view.

We could gather figs, bake bread, drink wine, I thought. We could fill a house with hungry and thirsty people, people ready to laugh again, and eat, and start something new. We could put flowers on the table. We could sing old songs.

I made it all the way to Sychar before I even noticed.

I'd left my water jar behind.

6

GOSPEL STORIES

I met Jesus at the dinner table. A vast, shaker-style oak, the three-leafed centerpiece of our modest family home had been handmade and special ordered to match a set of eight chairs my mother scored in a bargain at the legendary Woody's Chair Shop in Spruce Pine, North Carolina. "Woody" chairs are, to this day, constructed using a lathe and mortise machine from the 1800s and are held together without any nails or glue, just the shrinking and expanding of the wood. John F. Kennedy owned a Woody; there's one on display at the Smithsonian, another at the Metropolitan Museum of Fine Art. For two career educators, that dining set represented quite the splurge—eighty bucks a chair in 1984, according to my mother—so my parents gathered people around it every chance they got, filling their Woodys with hungry college students and friends from church, trimming the table with mismatched flatware and second-hand place mats.

It was at that table, over a steaming plate of spaghetti or pork chops or some other weekday meal, that I learned to pray, *"Jesus, thank you for Mommy and Daddy and Rachel and Amanda, and thank you for this food. Amen."* The first thing I knew about Jesus was that he was responsible for the existence of my parents, my sister, me, and my food. That seemed like good enough news to me.

It's funny that many of us who identify as "born-again Christians" can hardly remember our born-again experience, if at all. When my youth leader asked me, at age sixteen, to share my testimony at a Wednesday night youth gathering, I strained to conjure a single memory in which I "came to Jesus." From my first prayers at bedtime, to the picture books and songs that formed my early conceptions of the world, Jesus had always come to me, his presence as certain as dinner on the table and Mr. Rogers at noon.

Oh, I could tell of the sermon on hell that frightened me into my parents' bed at night, or of the day I asked my father to help me invite Jesus into my heart, or of my awkward plunge into the lukewarm water of the Faith Chapel baptistery—but none of those moments would tell the whole story. Had I looked beyond my immediate experience, I might also tell of those great-aunts and uncles who poured their liquor into the grass at Appalachian tent revivals, or my Lithuanian grandmother, who wrote a feisty letter to the pope explaining exactly why she converted to Protestantism. I could tell of Bible colleges and missionaries and reformations and abuses. I could tell of an African saint named Augustine who shaped a civilization's view of salvation, of a historic meal between a first-century Jew and a Gentile centurion, of a woman running breathlessly from an empty tomb. I'm sure I must have begun that high school testimony by saying I was "raised in a Christian home," without fully grasping the epic nature of this story to which I belonged.

That's what's so striking about the gospel, or "good news," of Jesus. It's a story at once grand and particular, sweeping and intimate. News that started as local gossip in a few sleepy fishing villages in ancient Palestine reverberated so profoundly through the centuries and across the world that it reached the ears of a pigtailed kindergartner in Birmingham, Alabama, in 1984. It reached Africa and India, the Andes and the Maldives, influencing ancient Roman soldiers, Irish farmers, Haitian fishermen, and Chinese school kids.

So what is this good news?

Well, it depends on who you ask.

For the apostle John, the gospel is the good news that in Jesus, God "became flesh and dwelt among us" (John 1:14 ESV), or more literally, God "became flesh and tabernacled—pitched a tent—among us." After all those years without a temple, and amid all the disputes about how and where to worship, God had taken up residence among the people by becoming one of us, Jesus himself serving as priest and sacrifice, holy festival and divine presence. "To those who believed in his name," John wrote, "he gave the right to become children of God—children born not of natural descent, nor of human decision or a husband's will, but born of God" (1:12–13).

For the woman at the well, the good news is she doesn't have to find the right temple after all, for God has started a new family of faith, beginning with despised Samaritans and the kind of women who do not belong at wells.

For Matthew and Mark, the good news is that Jesus is the long-awaited Messiah sent to establish God's reign on earth, not through conquest, power, and revenge, but through faithfulness, sacrifice, and unconditional love. The kingdom of heaven is not some far-off, future dream; it is here, among us, made real by the life, death, and resurrection of Jesus. Jesus is what it looks like when God is king, when God's will is done "on earth as it is in heaven."

To the Galilean children who annoyed the disciples by asking Jesus for a blessing, the good news is that Jesus is the kind of king who laughs at their jokes and tousles their hair.

To the physician Luke, the gospel is especially good news for the poor and oppressed, the disinherited and the sick. Defying nearly every culture's understanding of blessing, Jesus declared, "Blessed are you who are poor, for yours is the kingdom of God. Blessed are you who hunger now, for you will be satisfied. Blessed are you who weep now, for you will laugh" (Luke 6:20–21). Luke, more than any other gospel writer, shows that these promises of liberation are meant to be taken literally, that this is a God who rescues and heals and sets things right.

For the bleeding woman who spent her life's saving on doctors, the good news is Jesus touches those the law deems unclean in order to make them well.

The apostle Paul describes the gospel as the good news that, in Jesus, the story of Israel has reached its climax, and through him, the chosen people of God will finally fulfill their purpose of blessing the entire world with salvation. This means Gentiles have been "grafted in" to Israel's story, so any law or ritual that might keep them from full inclusion into God's family must be set aside for the sake of unity.

For the blind beggar, whom Jesus healed with a little dirt and water, the good news is pretty simple. "One thing I do know," he told the skeptical religious leaders, "I was blind but now I see!" (John 9:25).

The good news is as epic as it gets, with universal theological implications, and yet the Bible tells it from the perspective of fishermen and farmers, pregnant ladies and squirmy kids. This story about the nature of God and God's relationship to humanity smells like mud and manger hay and tastes like salt and wine. It is concerned, not simply with questions of eternity, but with paying taxes and filling bellies and addressing a woman's chronic menstrual complications. It is the biggest story and the smallest story all at once—the great quest for the One Ring and the quiet friendship of Frodo and Sam.

Much has been made in recent years about the value of rendering the gospel into a single, digestible aphorism. D. L. Moody claimed he could fit the gospel on a coin; I was once challenged to sum it up in a tweet. But it strikes me as fruitless to try and turn the gospel into a statement when God so clearly gave us a story—or, more precisely, a person.

Indeed, in Scripture, no two people encounter Jesus in exactly the same way. Not once does anyone pray the "Sinner's Prayer" or ask Jesus into their heart. The good news is good for the whole world, certainly, but what makes it good varies from person to person and community to community. Liberation from sin looks different for the rich young ruler than it does for the woman caught in adultery. The good news that Jesus is the Messiah has a different impact on John the Baptist, a Jewish prophet, than it does the Ethiopian eunuch, a Gentile and outsider. Salvation means one thing for Mary Magdalene, first to witness the resurrection, and another to the thief who died next to Jesus on a cross. The gospel is like a mosaic of stories, each one part of a larger story, yet beautiful and truthful on its own. There's no formula, no blueprint.

Flannery O'Connor once said, "A story is a way to say something that can't be said any other way, and it takes every word in the story to say what the meaning is. You tell a story because a statement would be inadequate. When anybody asks what a story is about, the only proper thing is to tell them to read the story."[1]

So when someone asks, "What is the gospel?" the best response is, "Let me tell you a story." You might start with Abraham, Isaiah, or Luke. You might start with the Samaritan woman at the well. You might start with a story about your grandmother or a rural church camp or a dining room table surrounded by Woody's chairs. At some point, you will get to Jesus, and Jesus will change everything.

There's a story in Matthew's and Mark's gospels about a woman who anoints Jesus with a jar of costly perfume in prophetic antici- pation of his impending arrest and crucifixion. When the disciples harass her for what they see as a waste of resources, Jesus defends the woman, declaring, "Truly I tell you, wherever the gospel is preached throughout the world, what she has done will also be told, in memory of her" (Mark 14:9). His response suggests that preaching the gospel means telling stories about the *life* of Jesus, not simply his death and resurrection. In the words of Pope Benedict XVI, "Jesus himself, the entirety of his acting, teaching, living, raising and remaining with us is the 'gospel.'"[2]

This is what the New Testament is about. It's the good news of Jesus told from multiple perspectives—"the gospel according to . . ." The books of Matthew, Mark, and Luke—often referred to as the Synoptic Gospels—tell the story through spiritual biography, drawing from eyewitness accounts, existing source material, and the authors' own memories to recall what Jesus did and taught. The book of John tells the story with a bit more creativity, adding new accounts and changing or embellishing details to make larger theological points about the significance of Jesus' life, death, and resurrection. The Acts of the Apostles describes the impact the good news had on thousands of people living in communities around the Mediterranean, and in particular on Paul, a devout Jew who initially sought to suppress the Christian movement but then had a dramatic conversion experience and became a critical advocate for the inclusion of Gentiles in God's redemption story. The Epistles, or letters, which comprise twenty-one of the twenty-seven "books" in the New Testament, give us a glimpse into how various first-century churches understood, debated, and applied the implications of the good news to their daily communal lives.

All told, the New Testament provides twenty-seven first- century documents testifying to what Jesus said and did, and to the impact he made on the doctors and fishermen, peasants and religious leaders, men and women, Jews, Samaritans, Africans, Greeks, and Romans who encountered him.

God did not see fit to print the gospel on a coin, so why should we?

When Jesus himself talks about the good news, he frames it primarily in terms of "the kingdom of God." Variations of this phrase (or it's counterpart, "the kingdom of heaven") occur eighty-two times in the Synoptic Gospels alone. As N. T. Wright and other New Testament scholars have shown, it's important to understand that kingdom terminology refers not to some faraway paradise filled with disembodied souls, but rather to the will and reign of God, unleashed into the world through the life, death, and resurrection of Jesus.

"*God's kingdom* in the preaching of Jesus," explained Wright, "refers not to postmortem destiny, not to our escape from this world into another one, but God's sovereign rule coming 'on earth as it is in heaven.' . . . Heaven, in the Bible, is not a future destiny but the other, hidden dimension of ordinary life—God's dimension, if you like. God made heaven and earth; at the last he will remake both and join them together forever."[3]

What this means precisely remains something of a mystery, for Jesus' favorite way to speak about the kingdom is through story, riddle, and metaphor.

The kingdom is like a treasure buried in a field; the man who discovers it sells all he owns to buy the field, for what does he have to lose?

The kingdom is like yeast that a woman took and mixed into three measures of flour until all of it was leavened.

It is the wheat growing in the midst of weeds, the net catching an abundance of fish, the pearl germinating in a sepulchral shell.[4]

The kingdom, Jesus taught, is right here—present yet hidden, immanent yet transcendent. It is at hand—among us and beyond us, now and not-yet. The kingdom of heaven, he said, belongs to the poor, the meek, the peacemakers, the merciful, and those who hunger and thirst for God. It advances not through power and might, but through missions of mercy, kindness, and humility. In this kingdom, many who are last will be first and many who are first will be last. The rich don't usually get it, Jesus said, but children always do. This is a kingdom whose savior arrives not on a warhorse, but a donkey, not through triumph and conquest, but through death and resurrection. This kingdom is the only kingdom that will last.

There is nothing Jesus talked about more than the kingdom. It is by far his favorite topic. "Jesus went through all the towns and villages," Matthew reported, "teaching in their synagogues, proclaiming the good news of the kingdom and healing every disease and sickness" (9:35).

And yet you'd never know it from the way many modern Christians talk about the gospel. "Jesus came to die," they often say, referring to a view of Christianity that reduces the gospel to a transaction, whereby God needed a spotless sacrifice to atone for the world's sins and thus sacrificed Jesus on the cross so believers could go to heaven. In this view, Jesus basically shows up to post our bail. His life and teachings make for an interesting backstory but prove largely irrelevant to the work of salvation. Dallas Willard called it "the gospel of sin management."[5]

What happened on the cross has been the subject of wonder and debate for centuries, with Christians of good faith employing different metaphors and language to articulate its significance, but any view that reduces Jesus to a sort of *deus ex machina*, necessary only for a single moment of rescue, strips the incarnation of all its power and tells a far simpler story than the one the Bible actually gives us. Jesus didn't just "come to die." Jesus came to live—to teach, to heal, to tell stories, to protest, to turn over tables, to touch people who weren't supposed to be touched and eat with people who weren't supposed to be eaten with, to break bread, to pour wine, to wash feet, to face temptation, to tick off the authorities, to fulfill Scripture, to forgive, to announce the start of a brand-new kingdom, to show us what that kingdom is like, to show us what God is like, to love his enemies to the point of death at their hands, and to beat death by rising from the grave.

Jesus did not simply die to save us from our sins; Jesus *lived* to save us from our sins. His life and teachings show us the way to liberation.

But you can't fit all that on a bumper sticker.

So we try to boil it down to a formula. Four steps. The "Romans Road." John 3:16. And yet the gospel itself, in its eternal scope and scandalous particularity, defies reduction.

Like it or not, the gospel is a story *unleashed*. Even Jesus had trouble keeping a lid on it. According to Matthew and Mark's accounts, Jesus often asked those he healed not to tell anyone about his miracles, but to no avail. Sure enough, the crowds got so big, Jesus had to flee to the desert to get some privacy. Jesus predicted the gospel would reach people from the east and the west, the north and the south; John described them coming from every tribe, every language, and every nation. There's just no way you can give this many people a story and expect them to stay "on message." The gospel fails rather epically at brand management.

And that makes some people nervous. That makes *me* nervous. Because it means every Christian gets a testimony, every Christian gets a "gospel according to . . ." whether you're Desmond Tutu or Tim Tebow.

Sometimes those gospel stories step on your toes. Sometimes they challenge or annoy. Sometimes they force you to confront your privilege, your pride, or your lack of imagination for just how reckless and wild and indiscriminate the Holy Spirit can be.

Ask my sister Amanda about the gospel and she will tell you a story about a field hospital outside of Mosul, Iraq, and about a nurse she met there who, after dressing the wounds of toddlers in the children's ward, wasn't sure she could do the same for the ISIS fighters in the enemy combatant ward. Amanda, who works for the relief organization Samaritan's Purse, will tell you about how this nurse did it anyway, tending to the ISIS fighters with as much care as she tended the children they had injured, cleaning their wounds, changing their bed pans, and holding their hands as they died. "To walk from a ward of innocent victims to a ward full of the perpetrators," Amanda wrote in an e-mail to me, "and to show equal love and service is not humanly possible. It's divine. It's the gospel."

Ask my friend Nadia Bolz-Weber about the gospel and she will tell you about alcoholism and rebellion and recovery meetings, about finding Jesus at rock bottom and surprising everyone by getting ordained. The six-foot-one, heavily tattooed Lutheran priest who cusses like a sailor and still does a bit of stand-up now and then will talk about starting a church in Denver for junkies and drag queens, doubters and survivors, and about how her job is "to point to Christ and to preach the gospel and to remind people that they're absolutely loved, that none of their f-ups are more powerful than God's mercy."[6]

Ask Sara Miles about the gospel, and she will tell you a story about how one day, when she was forty-six, she wandered into an unfamiliar church in San Francisco, ate a piece of bread, took a sip of wine, and experienced an "unexpected and terribly inconvenient Christian conversion." She will tell you about growing up atheist, enjoying a thoroughly secular life, and then, in a single moment, falling in love with "a religion rooted in the most ordinary yet subversive practice: a dinner table where everyone is welcome, where the despised and outcast are honored."[7] Sara would go on to partner with this church, Saint Gregory's of Nyssa Episcopal Church, to create a massive food pantry, one of the largest in the country, where the poor, elderly, sick, homeless, and marginalized from the community are served each week from the very table where she took her first communion—no questions asked, no strings attached.

Ask Augustine Assir, an Indian Christian from Chennai, about the gospel and he may tell you a story about translating for Mother Teresa or Billy Graham, but he is more likely to tell you about his ministry among the people in India's lowest castes—those suffering from poverty, leprosy, and HIV-AIDS—whom he and his wife, Hera, love like their own.

Ask the precocious first grader marching out of Vacation Bible School with a Jesus-themed coloring book under her arm and she will likely say, "The good news is Jesus loves me, this I know, for the Bible tells me so."

And she will be right.

They will all be right.

The gospel means that every small story is part of a sweeping story, every ordinary life part of an extraordinary movement. God is busy making all things new, and the life, death, and resurrection of Jesus has opened that work to everyone who wants in on it. The church is not a group of people who believe all the same things; the church is a group of people caught up in the same story, with Jesus at the center.

There's a great scene in Oscar Wilde's play *Salome* when King Herod receives reports that Jesus of Nazareth has been raising the dead.

"I do not wish him to do that," cries Herod. "I forbid him to do that. I allow no man to raise the dead. This man must be found and told that I forbid him to raise the dead."

It's the classic bluster of a tyrant, threatened, like Xerxes, by something he can't control.

"Where is this man?" Herod demands of his servant.

"He is in every place, my lord," replies the courtier, "but it is hard to find Him."[8]

Two thousand years and two billion followers later, one thing is clear: there's no such thing as *just* a story.

～

We spend a lot of time speculating about what God is like. We argue about it, build theologies around it, sometimes even wage war over it. We use words like *omniscient* and *omnipotent, sovereign* and *trinitarian* to describe a God who defies language and eclipses metaphor. I once sat at a bar between two seminary students hotly debating God's supposed *immutability,* accusations of heresy and *supersessionism* flying at one another with their spittle, their breath smelling of pretzels and beer. When nestled in my La-Z-Boy with a new theology book, its austere weight a comfort blanket to my ego, it can be easy to imagine God as a set of ideas, a philosophy, or a system of thought.

And yet the scandal of the gospel is that one day the God of our theology books and religious debates showed up—as a person, in flesh and blood. And while God indeed delivered a few sermons and entertained a couple of theological discussions, it is notable that according to the Gospels, when God was wrapped in flesh and walking among us, the single most occupying activity of the Creator of the universe, the Ultimate Reality, the Alpha and Omega and the great I AM of ages past and ages to come, was to tell stories.

Lots and lots and lots of stories.

Matthew reported that Jesus spoke to the crowds in parables and "did not say anything to them without using a parable" (13:34).

The movies always make it seem as though people were drawn

to Jesus by some mysterious force beyond their control, a gravitational pull accompanied by swelling strings and warm light. But to me the appeal of Jesus seems a lot more concrete: this was a man who loved a good feast and could spin a good tale. Of course people craved his presence.

With his parables, Jesus invites his listeners to see the kingdom of God in the images and dramas of everyday life—in a woman baking bread, a group of bridesmaids preparing for a wedding, a roadside mugging, a lost coin, a lost sheep, a lost son. Some parables are just a sentence or two long, barely more than a metaphor. Others include multiple characters, locations, and themes. While they are rooted in the commonplace, it is a mistake to label these stories *simple*. Jesus told rich, compelling tales, including one about a moneylender who forgave two wildly unequal debts, another about a persistent widow who nagged a judge into granting her justice, and another about a banquet in which all were invited but only the poor and sick and forgotten remembered to come. By employing dramatic reversals, wherein a penitent tax collector was granted God's mercy over an accomplished Pharisee and a despised Samaritan helped his suffering Jewish neighbor, Jesus used parables to provoke and surprise.

Unfortunately, our familiarity with these often-told tales can numb us to their provocations, which are rooted in an ancient honor-shame culture, yet have survived the centuries to make frequent appearances in children's sermons and watered-down morality tales. It may be touching, though unremarkable, to us that the father welcomed his prodigal son home with open arms when, unlike the first people to hear that story, we don't live in a culture where the disavowal of an inheritance is akin to wishing one's father dead. We fondly praise the "good Samaritans" in our midst without realizing that in making a Samaritan the hero of his story, Jesus was centering a religious and ethnic minority ostracized by his first-century Jewish community. (*The Cotton Patch Gospel*, which recasts the stories of Jesus into the language and culture of the mid-twentieth-century South, renders the unfortunate traveler as a stranded white motorist, ignored by a white preacher and a white choir director, only to be rescued by a black truck driver. A comparable story from today might make a Muslim immigrant the hero.)

Of course, many parables remain confounding, perhaps especially to modern American readers. The parable of the workers in the vineyard, wherein a vineyard owner pays those who worked from sunup to sundown the same wage he pays the workers who show up for an hour, an illustration of God's unscrupulous grace, always offends my overwrought sense of fairness, even though I know that's kind of the point. The story of the rich man and Lazarus, a fanciful tale in which a poor beggar is welcomed into paradise after his death while the rich neighbor who ignored his suffering suffers in flames, a "great chasm" fixed forever between them, can jolt us out of our normal theologizing about faith, works, justice, and grace.

The gospel of Mark includes the enticing detail that Jesus privately explained the meaning of the more mysterious parables to his disciples, and yet we are privy to very few of these explanations ourselves (Mark 4:34). While some parables invite rather straightforward interpretations, others include multiple layers, soliciting a diversity of reactions and engagements, depending on the audience. Apparently, some parables are meant to keep us guessing.

"When we seek universal morals from a genre that is designed to surprise, challenge, shake up, or indict," wrote Amy-Jill Levine of the parables, "and look for a single meaning in a form that opens to multiple interpretations, we are necessarily limiting the parables, and, so, ourselves. . . . We might be better off thinking less about what [the parables] 'mean,' and more about what they can 'do': remind, provoke, refine, confront, disturb."[9]

Volumes could be written about the parables alone, of course. Indeed, many volumes have. These stories within the Story beg for dramatic reenactment and spirited debate. They inspire imaginative retellings.

But what I love most about the parables are the details. I love that when the lost sheep is found, the shepherd "joyfully puts it on his shoulders" and carries it all the way home (Luke 15:5). I love that when the father greets his prodigal son upon return, he meets him halfway down the road with an embrace and a sloppy kiss. I love that Jesus knew you can't sew a patch of shrunk cloth on an old garment or the patch will pull away, and that you can't pour new wine into old wineskins or the skins will burst. I love that he described the kingdom of God as a tiny mustard seed that grows into a great tree with branches wide enough and strong enough to welcome all "the birds of the air" (Matthew 13:32 ESV). I love these details because they reveal to me a God who is immersed in creation, deeply embedded within the lives of God's beloved. Ours is a God who knows how to mend clothes and bake bread, a God familiar with the planting and harvest seasons, the traditions of bridesmaids, and the tickle of wool on the back of the neck.

Episcopal priest and gourmet chef Robert Farrar Capon says the parables show us that the Bible "is not about someplace else called heaven, nor about somebody at a distance called God. Rather it is about *this place here*, in all its *this*ness, and placiness, and about the intimate and immediately Holy One who, *at no distance from us at all*, moves mysteriously to make creation true both to itself and to him."[10]

For all our lofty ruminations about God, for all the symphonies and theologies and liturgies for the divine, I've yet to find a more profound expression of God's nature than the one that begins, "Once upon a time, there was a shepherd and a lost sheep."

God With Us is a marvelous storyteller.

෬

"There is deliverance in the music, there is healing in the music, there is love—there is *love*—in the music."

Tiffany Thomas had reached a crescendo. As the twenty-nine-year-old pastor concluded her riveting and rhythmic testimony about how the hymns of the black church drew her to Jesus, the nine hundred people crammed into Saint Mark's Cathedral in Minneapolis rose to their feet and cheered.

That weekend, a dozen speakers, ranging from pastors to artists to teachers to scientists joined Tiffany in responding to the question, *Why Christian?* Why, with all the atrocities past and present committed in God's name, amid all the divisions ripping apart the church, in spite of all their doubts and frustrations and fears about faith, are they still followers of Jesus? What makes them continue to believe?

My friend Nadia Bolz-Weber and I posed the question at our inaugural "Why Christian?" conference in 2015 because it's a question that weighs on us every day and it's a question Christians don't ask one another often enough. As each speaker approached the microphone to share their stories—some with the practiced cadence of working preachers, others with a quiet vulnerability, and all with the conviction of people whose faith has been hard-won—it became clear that there simply remains no greater apologetic for the Christian faith than a life caught up in the story of Jesus.

"I am a Christian," explained Episcopal priest Kerlin Richter, "because having a body wasn't always good news for me, but then

I met Good News that had a body. In Jesus, I met a God who spits and kisses, who yells and cries. I am a messy and embodied person, and this is a messy and embodied faith."

"I am a Christian," declared Austin Channing Brown, an author and activist whose work focuses on racial justice in the church, "because God knows my pain, not in an abstract way, but in a real, bloody, enfleshed way."

"I am a Christian," said Rachel Murr, a researcher and counselor, "because the gospel is good news for gay people too."

"I am a Christian," explained Baptist preacher and human rights activist Allyson Robinson, "because I don't always know if this story is true, but I choose to live my life as if it were. I choose to live as if the things Jesus died for were worthy of God's sacrifice and therefore worthy of mine."

We were a diverse group: evangelical and Lutheran, Baptist and Episcopalian, Latina and black and white and Indian and Korean, high church and low church, Catholic and Protestant, Reformed and Methodist, straight and gay and bisexual and transgender, pastors and scholars, writers and activists, crunchy dreadlocked mamas, tattooed and foul-mouthed priests, sweet-talkin' southerners, and stiletto-boasting fashionistas. Looking at us from the outside, you'd have no idea what we all had in common. While there were variations in the verses, our shared refrain remained unapologetically orthodox, undeniably Christian. We spoke of sin, repentance, baptism, confession, incarnation, resurrection, and Scripture. We proclaimed the great mystery of the faith—that Christ has died, Christ has risen, and Christ will come again. We served and received communion. We ran out of tissue.

When it came time for me to share, I spoke honestly about my doubts about the Bible and Christianity. I confessed my uncertainties about raising children in this broken and beloved community we call the church. I explained how gatherings like these help restore my faith because they pull me out of my head and into the lives of others, into the big, colorful, messy, and magical story of Jesus.

"I am a Christian," I concluded, "because the story of Jesus is still the story I'm willing to risk being wrong about."

I had forgotten the power of giving testimony, of publicly recounting our unique "gospels according to . . ." We can know a person for decades, share a pew with them in church every Sunday, without ever knowing their testimonies, without ever asking them, "Hey, why Christian?" We can spend a lifetime singing hymns and reading the Bible without honestly answering that question for ourselves.

Jesus invites us into a story that is bigger than ourselves, bigger than our culture, bigger even than our imaginations, and yet we get to tell that story with the scandalous particularity of our particular moment and place in time. We are storytelling creatures because we are fashioned in the image of a storytelling God. May we never neglect the gift of that. May we never lose our love for telling the tale.

THE SEA

(A Choose-Your-Own-Adventure Story)

*W*ham.

Brother Matt's elbow meets your sweaty temple just as the guitar drops off and the boat full of tourists break into an a cappella chorus of "How Great Is Our God." So lost in the reverie of his "God moment" (you were told by the tour guides to expect many of these), Brother Matt doesn't seem to notice the blow. He just extends his arms over his head in worship and continues to sing out of tune, his body odor reaching your nostrils just as the converted fishing vessel lurches forward and you catch another spray of cold water from the Sea of Galilee.

There are far too many people on this boat.

You consider scooting an inch to your right, but that would land you directly into the lap of Brother Mark's wife, an exceedingly devout woman whose name you can never remember but whose Bible, prayer journal, sun hat, and disposable camera leave little room for company. She, too, is looking at the northern horizon, where a black cloud looms, the blue-green water below it speckled with whitecaps.

Brother Andy, the self-appointed worship leader, transitions to the opening chord progression for "Oceans," to much applause. Though the Sea of Galilee is technically a freshwater lake, the song resonates emotionally, and "God moments" ensue. You scan the deck for a barf bag or a life vest, or both. The captain, a skinny Israeli who speaks little English, seems unconcerned by the darkening sky. He's kicked off the engine and lit a cigarette, smiling like a young man who's convinced a group of Southern Baptists from Alabama to rent a tour boat by the hour. The mountainous shoreline might as well be a million miles away.

You regret the falafels you ate for lunch. You regret wearing jeans instead of shorts. You regret never taking swimming lessons as a kid. You regret everything, really—this trip, your ordination, the last decade of ministry. A pilgrimage to the Holy Land was supposed to straighten you out—everyone said it would, but you've never felt more disconnected from God, more like a tourist to your own faith. A dozen selfies from as many holy sites can't change the frightening reality you've been hiding from your church: You are a pastor who isn't sure he believes in God anymore. You are a pastor who hiked up the Mount of Olives, strolled through the garden of Gethsemane, waded through the Jordan River, and felt . . . *nothing*.

"Hey, Pete. Pastor Pete! Why aren't you singing?"

Matt is peering into your face, and you catch your beleaguered reflection in his sunglasses.

"Oh, I'm just tired," you shout over the wind. "Maybe a little queasy."

Matt slaps you on the back and laughs.

"It's all good, brother! It's all good."

He always says that. About everything. It will probably go on his tombstone.

You remember with relief the dimenhydrinate you stashed in your back pocket on the way out of the hotel room that morning. Your trembling fingers manage to find the bottle and unscrew the childproof lid. You swallow two pills without water, then add a third for good measure. Sure, the nausea treatment makes you a little loopy, but it saved your life during that awful van ride with the youth on their ski retreat a few years ago. You put your head in your hands, close your eyes, and imagine the stillness of your hotel room, the cool of your pillow. In just a few hours, you can rest. In just a few hours you will at last be left alone. Thank God you paid extra to avoid a roommate.

When you open your eyes, you can't believe how dark it is. Dusk is descending swiftly on account of the coming storm. The water, mountains, and horizon blend into a hazy, foreboding gray. Andy's music sheets blow overboard, and for once, the group falls silent. Matt pushes his sunglasses to the top of his head.

"We probably oughta think about headin' back," he observes, to no one in particular.

A crack of thunder finally gets the captain's attention. He tosses his cigarette off the port bow, revs up the engine, and turns the boat toward Tiberias. You head out against the wind, leaping over the waves.

Whether from the effects of the dimenhydrinate or the adverse weather conditions, you cannot know, but everything moves as if in slow motion from that point on, the shoreline appearing as far away after what seems like an hour as when the tour boat first turned back. Heavy raindrops assail the open deck. Lightning strikes somewhere on shore. You surrender to the hypnotic, throbbing drone of engine and waves. At some point, Mark's wife—her name is Reba, or Rhoda maybe—drops her things, staggers to the gunwale, and releases the contents of her lunch into the churning water below. As the sky grows darker, the faces around you grow paler.

There are far too many people on this boat.

Suddenly, you spot something strange amid the whitecaps off the starboard—a figure, about a hundred feet away, steady in the tumult. You squint, shielding your eyes from the rain with your hand. *A statue of some kind? A buoy?*

The captain cuts the engine. Perhaps he has seen it too. The boat bobs violently about, wind and rain obscuring your view. You stumble to the bow to get a better look.

It can't be. Or can it?

A man! Standing in, or rather *on*, the water!

Ghostlike, he wears a loose white robe that ripples in the wind. From here he looks Israeli, with long dark hair and a beard. The figure takes a few more steps forward, stops, and then calmly waves an arm to signal the boat. He must be eighty feet away . . .

Now seventy-five . . .

Now seventy.

Is it he or the boat that is moving?

Your mind rushes through the possibilities—shallow water, holographic projection, some kind of practical joke the Galileans like to play on Southern Baptists. You're wearing your contacts, and the prescription's up to date. You turn to the other passengers, whose shorts and T-shirts are now soaked. They, too, are looking starboard, stunned.

The man keeps walking closer and closer, wind behind him, right arm outstretched. He must be fewer than forty feet away.

You can hardly believe it when the words rise to your throat and out of your mouth:

"Is that . . . you, Lord?"

Immediately the question gets caught in the wind, and you're glad. *What could you be thinking? You don't even believe this stuff anymore.*

And yet somehow, amid the roar of the storm, the figure answers back, clear as if it were a cloudless spring morning.

"Don't be afraid."

You feel it stirring the way it stirred in you as a boy when you walked the train tracks over the river gorge: that overwhelming, irrational, exhilarating impulse to screw it all and *jump.* Your grip on the gunwale loosens. Your right foot finds the rail. You glance at the dark water below, then back up at the man in white.

If you jump, go to Adventure A.

If you stay in the boat, go to Adventure B.

꙳

Adventure A

Splash!

The water shocks with cold. For a moment, you think you've gone under, but once you steady yourself, you see you are standing, submerged only to your knees. The waves beat relentlessly against your body, threatening to knock you over. Upon what you stand you cannot know—a rock? a sandbar? the sea itself? Your legs are numb, jeans heavy and wet; you cannot feel your feet. You search through the rain for the man in white and catch a blur of him up ahead.

"Come to me!" he shouts.

The first step toward him is the hardest, like descending unfamiliar stairs in the dark. You push your leg against the current and into the abyss, reaching and reaching and reaching, before finally finding your footing. Then you take the next step and the next and the next. With each one, your spirit grows calmer, your heart lighter. To your surprise, you begin to laugh. Around you the storm rages on, but you feel like a kid at a water park; you feel like you did when you were young and it was easy. At last you've escaped all the pressure, all the doubt, all those dumb, expectant faces on the boat. At last you are free.

You search again for the man in white and are surprised he seems just as far away as when you jumped out of the boat, maybe thirty feet. Only now you can make out his face, and it's not what you expect. Instead of serenity and encouragement, his expression is one of . . . puzzlement, surprise. Jesus looks concerned.

And that's when you remember.

It strikes you with the same force as when you realize you've left your luggage on the plane or when you wake up the morning after someone has died and remember they are gone:

You can't swim.

Immediately comes the sensation of sleep-falling, only it won't stop. You just keep falling and falling and falling, water rushing through your nose and mouth, arms and legs flailing. Every time you resurface, you get knocked back by a wave. Every time you get knocked back by a wave, your limbs grow heavier and it's harder to fight. Your chest begins to burn, the light around you narrowing. You long for the surface but can't remember if it's up or down, an inch or a hundred miles away. Surprise gives way to panic, panic to surrender.

What a stupid way to die.

Then, after what seems like a lifetime, a tug on the neck of your shirt, an arm around your chest. Up you go until finally you break the surface, where you gasp violently for air. You can't seem to get enough. Heart throbbing, chest aching, every orifice burns as your body is dragged to shore. The minute your knees hit the sand, you collapse into the shallow water and vomit, while above you, a large, panting beast of a man, soaked in his Jesus Saves T-shirt, pats your back reassuringly and says, "It's all good, brother. It's all good."

It will take a while to put the pieces together, and even then some details remain fuzzy. No one from the group saw you jump; they were so distracted by the wind and waves and by the Israeli deckhand waving the boat in from the pier, wearing a white poncho and shouting directions at the captain. The storm had taken out all the lights. Matt spotted you just before your head went under, and without even thinking about it, threw his 270-pound, former-linebacker body over the rails and into the sea. He had you to the shore before the first tourist disembarked the boat.

Even after you hear the story a dozen times, you cannot believe this is the sum of it, that something more didn't happen that night. And yet your only proof is the fact that the surrender you felt when walking toward Jesus—or that deckhand, or whomever—hasn't gone away. You feel a little foolish, certainly, but you feel unburdened somehow, free.

"I think I owe you my life," you tell Matt the next morning at breakfast.

"You don't owe me a thing," he replies, jovial as ever. "I know you would have done the same thing for me."

And somehow, despite all evidence to the contrary, you believe.

⌒⌒

Adventure B

Splash!

You hear it just seconds after you put everything together—the darkened shoreline, the wave-assailed pier, the Israeli deckhand wearing a white poncho signaling at the boat from the jetty.

But Brother Matt has already jumped overboard, his imposing, 270-pound frame now bobbing precariously in the waves. He attempts to swim toward the pier, but his stroke is awkward, overwrought. His head slips under the water, then back up again.

"Help!" he shouts, his voice small in the tempest.

You look back at your comrades in the boat, who sit paralyzed with shock and fear. The captain is navigating the vessel to dock, the deckhand scrambling for a rope. Matt goes under the water again, and you know there's no time to spare. Pushing back thoughts of those thwarted swim lessons, you leap over the gunwale and into the sea.

The impact shocks your body with cold. For a moment, you think you've gone under, but once you steady yourself, you realize, to your amazement, you're standing. The water is only as high as your calves! Upon what you stand you cannot know—a rock? a sandbar? the sea itself? The pier is at least thirty feet away. Your legs are numb, jeans heavy and wet; you cannot feel your feet.

You scour the tumult for Matt and see his sunglasses floating up ahead.

The first step is the hardest, like descending unfamiliar stairs in the dark. You push your leg against the current and into the abyss, reaching and reaching, before finally finding your footing. Then you take the next step and the next and the next. With each one, your spirit grows calmer, your purpose clearer. The storm rages around you, but the fear washes off of you with the rain. You almost laugh.

Then a hand grasps your ankle. You kneel down to grab hold of Matt's arm and suddenly find yourself neck-deep in the water, assailed by Matt's frantic thrashing and the relentless pounding of waves. He resurfaces for a moment, gasping for air.

"Matt! It's okay!" you shout, treading water like a lifeguard who's done it a million times. "It's all good, brother. Be calm."

Matt relaxes long enough for you to swim behind him and slide your arms under his. You grab his shoulders, tilt his body back so he can breathe, and make your way to the shore. It's as though you've acquired muscle memory for an activity you've never done before.

You have no idea how long you swim before you are met by Mark, Andy, and Phil, who help pull Matt to shore.

"I thought it was Jesus," Matt cries between coughs once you reach the beach.

"Me too, brother," you assure him.

As the story gets told over and over again in the intervening days, on tour buses and at restaurants, at the Church of the Holy Sepulchre and the Dome of the Rock, no one says anything about walking on water, and you don't mention it. Perhaps it was the dimenhydrinate, or some kind of adrenaline-infused temporary superpower. Perhaps you imagined it altogether. Who knows? All you know for certain is that the freedom you felt while standing amid all that chaos, all that wind and water and rain, has mysteriously remained. You haven't got your faith figured out—not by a long shot—but you've made peace with that. You jumped when it mattered.

Of course that doesn't keep you from sticking to your beach towel while the rest of the crew dashes to the water to float on their backs in the Dead Sea. You've had enough God moments for a while.

7

FISH STORIES

So what's the one Bible story you'll never preach a sermon on?"
I popped a cube of cheddar in my mouth and washed it down with some red wine. An introvert with dubious people skills, I spend most social gatherings exactly like this—camped out by the buffet table, asking inappropriate religious and political questions of whatever poor schmuck dares strike up a conversation with me. Fortunately, this was an event for Episcopal clergy, and if I have anything in common with Episcopal clergy, it's a fondness for cheese, wine, and inappropriate religious and political questions. I fit right in.

"Oh, without a question, it's the story about the fish with the coin in its mouth," said the priest, referring to the time Jesus paid his temple tax by instructing Peter to go to the lake, cast out a line, and remove a four-drachma coin from the mouth of the first fish he caught.

"It's weird enough trying to preach a sermon about taxes," said the priest, who serves a wealthy parish in Virginia. "That story just makes it weirder."

I laughed, for indeed the Bible includes some strange miracle stories, and many of the strangest have scales. In addition to the miracle of the fishy tax payment, there's the one where Jesus takes five loaves of bread and two fish and transforms them into a feast to feed five thousand, with baskets of leftovers to spare. Then there's the story of how Jesus called his first disciples by instructing a group of discouraged fishermen to try casting their nets into the sea one more time. When they skeptically oblige, they are rewarded with a draught so epic it breaks their nets and nearly sinks their boat. "Follow me," Jesus says, "and I will make you fishers of men" (Matthew 4:19 ESV).

Of course, all these tales are eclipsed by what may be the greatest fish story of all time: the story of Jonah, the Old Testament prophet tossed overboard, swallowed by a giant fish, kept alive in its belly for three days, and then coughed up onto shore, all so God could reach the people of Nineveh with forgiveness. To this epic tale Jesus likened his own three-day stint inside a tomb, calling his resurrection "the sign of the prophet Jonah" (Matthew 12:39–40). Is it any wonder that the first symbol of the Christian faith wasn't the cross, but rather the *ichthys*—the sign of a fish?

Now, I hail from Dayton, Tennessee, home of Lake Chickamauga, where a few years ago an angler named Gabe Keen landed a 15.3-pound largemouth bass, shattering a sixty-year-old state record. Our fishing here is legendary, drawing thousands of anglers for tournaments every summer and flushing our local economy with much-needed cash. I've seen people pull catfish out of those muddy waters that would give Leviathan a scare. I've also heard more than a few fish stories in my time. Dine at a local restaurant during bass season and you'll pick up all sorts of tall tales about the one that broke the line and got away—or better yet, the one that ate the one that broke the line and got away.

Sometimes the miraculous moments in Scripture strike me as those kinds of fish stories—colorful exaggerations of events that may or may not have transpired as recounted. In addition to being an introvert with dubious people skills, I'm a dependable skeptic, cautious of attributing supernatural causes to ordinary events. I've watched far too many people of strong faith succumb to illness and tragedy to believe God rewards the righteous with miraculous intervention with any sort of routine regularity. While it's plausible to me that the Holy Spirit moved with special urgency during Jesus' ministry and as the gospel spread throughout Asia Minor, the stories of Jesus healing the sick and walking on water, and of the apostles raising the dead and casting out demons, are some of the hardest of the New Testament for me to believe, and I know I'm not alone.

Some will argue that the Bible's miracle stories render the whole thing intellectually untenable, proving only the gullible and uneducated believe the Bible to be true. Others attempt to rationalize the miracle stories by developing elaborate, scientifically plausible explanations for them, whereby Lazarus suffers a cataleptic fit, the wise men spot a rare triple planetary conjunction, and Peter walks a conveniently located sandbank in the Sea of Galilee. Still others spiritualize every apparent miracle as strictly metaphorical, from the virgin birth to the healing of the blind and deaf to the resurrection of Jesus. And of course, many insist that only a literal interpretation of all these events will do.

Growing up, my conservative evangelical culture insisted on the latter, with one's confidence in the factuality of the Bible's miracle stories an important test of faith. Belief in the authority of Scripture required belief in its scientific and historical veracity, so if the Bible says the sun stood still for twenty-four hours, then that's exactly what happened. The earth stopped rotating and the sun froze in the sky; end of story. Often I was reminded of Jesus' words to Thomas that "blessed are those who have not seen and yet have believed" (John 20:29). One cannot be selective about which biblical miracles you believe, I was told, when they're all essentially the same.

Later, as a young adult, I would see the appeal of metaphorical interpretations, both at a scientific level and a literary one. The story of Jonah reads more like a parable than history, employing fanciful literary conventions and language, so why impose literalism on a text when the genre doesn't seem to demand it? And yet the epistles of Paul and the accounts of Luke, whether you believe them or not, purport a different purpose and employ a different literary style than Jonah, so it seems just as disingenuous to impose metaphor where those authors likely presumed fact. Furthermore, I had a hard time believing that a religion so concerned with bodies, ritual, suffering, and sustenance would produce a Messiah interested only in spiritual transformation and not physical transformation, when in Judaism the two are inextricably linked.

I once attended a lecture given by a Christian theologian who rejected the notion of the physical resurrection of Jesus in favor of a spiritualized interpretation wherein Jesus simply rose from the dead "in his disciples' hearts." Just as Jesus lives on in our collective memory, he argued, so friends and family do not literally rise from the dead but rather gain "eternal life" whenever we honor their legacy.

After the lecture, I turned to the person next to me, a black pastor who had been fidgeting anxiously throughout the hour, and asked what he thought.

"If the resurrection is about getting raised in memories and hearts," he said, "that's not very good news for me or my people. What does spiritual resurrection mean for all the brothers who died on slave ships and all the women lying in unmarked plantation graves? Where's their justice? Where's their liberation?

"If there's one thing historic Christianity is clear on," he said, "it's that bodies matter to God. A revolution without bodies isn't a revolution."

Of course, this pastor was speaking for himself and not necessarily all African Americans of faith, but I found his point persuasive. What makes the Bible's miracle stories so compelling is the idea that God cares about people's suffering, not simply their "spiritual blindness" or "spiritual poverty" but also their actual blindness and actual poverty. The apostle Paul insisted to the Corinthian church that the physical resurrection of Jesus, as witnessed by more than five hundred people, portends the resurrection of all who have died, all who have suffered, and that without it "our preaching is useless and so is your faith" (1 Corinthians 15:14).

And so I found myself dissatisfied with both sweeping literalism on the one hand and disembodied abstractions on the other.

It wasn't until churches started asking me for homilies based on the lectionary that I began really looking for answers. The Revised Common Lectionary assigns specific biblical texts for each week of the liturgical year, working through much of the New Testament over a three-year cycle, so when I visited these churches on speaking tour, I couldn't fall back on my old, polished lectures, but instead had to preach from "the text," which might bring me to Jesus casting out demons one Sunday, Jesus cursing the fig tree the next, Jesus walking on water the next. In order to offer a meaningful word to these congregations, I had to figure out what these stories were actually about.

In my research, I learned that while the gospel writers certainly emphasize the physicality of sickness, suffering, feeding, and healing, there is more going on in these stories than simple transmission of fact. For example, in Mark and Matthew's gospels, the feeding of the five thousand is followed by a nearly identical miracle just two chapters later, in which Jesus again multiplies food but starts with a different number of loaves and fishes, feeds a different number of followers, and produces a different number of basketfuls each time.

These numbers must be significant because in Mark's gospel, Jesus quizzes the disciples about them on a boat ride to Bethsaida.

"When I broke the five loaves for the five thousand, how many basketfuls of pieces did you pick up?" he asks as they sail out across the Sea of Galilee.

"Twelve," they reply.

"And when I broke the seven loaves for the four thousand, how many basketfuls of pieces did you pick up?"

"Seven," they answer.

"Do you still not understand?" Jesus asks (Mark 8:19–21).

And that's the end of it. The question just hangs there.

Reading along, one might respond, "Well no, actually, I don't understand. What am I missing?"

In Judaism, certain numbers carry special theological significance, and most scholars believe the numbers in these stories symbolically underscore the expansion of Jesus' ministry from the Jewish community to the greater Gentile world. The number twelve recalls the twelve tribes of Israel and is often employed in Scripture to refer to the Jewish people. (Remember: Jesus began his ministry with twelve disciples.) The number seven carries Gentile connotations and also signifies "fullness" or "completion." This interpretation finds support in the fact that the first miracle took place in a Jewish neighborhood near the Sea of Galilee, whereas the second occurred in the Decapolis, a Gentile area. The point, then, is that Jesus intends to feed and bless not just the Jews, but also the Gentiles, thus bringing to fruition God's promise to Abraham that through his people the entire world would be blessed. The bread in this case represents both physical and spiritual sustenance, its miraculous multiplication reminiscent of God's provision of manna to the liberated Hebrews, only this time made available to all who hunger.[1]

Such a reading might seem unnecessarily complicated, but the gospel writers intentionally direct us to the details. They want us to pay attention to them.

We see similar allusions at work in the episode of Jesus cursing the fig tree. As the story goes, Jesus and his disciples are headed toward Jerusalem from Bethany when they come upon a fruitless fig tree. No one is particularly surprised, as it isn't the season for figs. But Jesus, it seems, is hungry. So he curses the tree, saying, "May you never bear fruit again!" and according to Matthew's account, the tree immediately withers (Matthew 21:18–22). In Mark's account, the disciples only noticed the withered tree on their way back from Jerusalem (Mark 11:12–25).

What's going on here? What's the point of this curse? Is this just what happens when God-in-flesh gets "hangry"? Or does it mean, as one clever counterprotest sign posits, "God Hates Figs"?

In Hebrew Scripture, fig trees and vines symbolize plenty and peace, but when the Babylonians were threatening invasion and the people of Israel ignored the prophets' calls for repentance, Jeremiah warned that God would "take away their harvest. . . . There will be no grapes on the vine. There will be no figs on the tree, and their leaves will wither" (Jeremiah 8:13). Perhaps this imagery was on Jesus' mind as he traveled to Jerusalem that day. In Mark's account, the story of the fig tree bookends the story of Jesus' cleansing of the temple, suggesting the curse illustrates his frustration with Israel's fruitlessness and foreshadows his impending rejection by its religious and political leaders.

Often the key to unlocking the deeper meaning of a miracle story lies in Hebrew Scripture. Many of Jesus' actions serve as living, breathing reenactments of biblical images and prophecies. When Jesus entered Jerusalem, for example, he chose to ride through the city on the back of a donkey in order to fulfill Zechariah's vision of a king who comes to Zion, "righteous and victorious, lowly and riding on a donkey" (9:9). Many scholars believe Jesus' calming of the stormy sea and his exorcising of the Gerasene demoniac together function as a sort of double fulfillment story based on Psalm 65:7, which declares that God "stilled the roaring of the seas, the roaring of their waves, and the turmoil of the nations." In Scripture the sea represents chaos, its churning, unpredictable waters teeming with monsters and demons, threatening death. So when Jesus rebukes the stormy sea, when he commands its fish and walks on its waves, he's not just showing off; he's making a statement about the God who reigns over even our most visceral, primal fears, the God who, in the words of the psalmist, "makes a way in the sea, a path in the mighty waters" (Isaiah 43:16 ESV). "Take courage!" Jesus tells the dumbfounded disciples as he walks across the sea. "It is I. Don't be afraid" (Matthew 14:27). The best translation of "It is I" from the Greek is "I AM"—a clear reference to the God of Abraham and Isaac, Moses and Miriam.

Throughout the New Testament, Jesus "acts out" biblical stories and images in order to infuse them with new meaning and point to himself as their ultimate fulfillment. Far from abstracting the redemptive themes of Scripture, Jesus seems intent on putting flesh on them.

Even the healing miracles, which undoubtedly reveal Christ's compassion for the suffering, carry a deeper theological message. The gospel of Mark includes three stories that make this plain.

In the first, a man with leprosy comes to Jesus, falls on his knees, and begs him for help, pleading, "If you are willing, you can make me clean" (Mark 1:40). In the first century, leprosy could refer to a number of different skin conditions, including the disfiguring infectious disease for which the word is used today. In Jesus' culture, anyone regarded as a leper faced intense social and religious stigmatization, for not only did the condition make a person potentially contagious; it also rendered them ritually unclean, or nonkosher. This meant exclusion from corporate worship in the temple and rejection from communal life. According to the book of Leviticus, simply touching someone with leprosy results in physical and spiritual contamination.

When Jesus sees the leper, he responds emotionally. Some translations say he was "moved by compassion"; others report he was "indignant," likely over the man's unjust treatment. Regardless, Mark chose his next words carefully: Jesus "reached out his hand and touched the man," and immediately the man was healed (v. 41).

The second story describes a woman who suffered from what appears to be a chronic uterine hemorrhage. "She had suffered a great deal under the care of many doctors and had spent all she had," Mark noted, "yet instead of getting better she grew worse" (5:26). (What a sad and stark description of life with chronic illness.) Awful as this condition already was, it was made worse by the fact that the law prevented physical contact with menstruating women and considered them ritually impure for the duration of their periods and seven days after. This woman's continual bleeding rendered her perpetually untouchable, cut off from her husband, her community, and her temple.

Perhaps she had heard about Jesus healing the man with leprosy, for in this account she garners the courage to join a large crowd following Jesus through the city streets, pressing in around him.

"If I just touch his clothes," she resolves, "I will be healed" (v. 28). So she stretches out her arm, and in an act of defiance, touches Jesus' cloak with her fingertips. Mark reported that "immediately her bleeding stopped; and she felt in her body that she was free from her suffering" (v. 29).

Jesus, sensing "the power had gone out from him," stops and asked who touched him. His disciples remind him they are in the midst of a mob at the moment, so there's no way to know. But the woman, "trembling with fear," falls before Jesus and tells him what happened (vv. 33–34).

Jesus responds with tenderness. "Daughter," he says, "your faith has healed you" (v. 34).

In the third story, which Mark dramatically interwove with the story of the hemorrhaging woman, a religious leader named Jairus rushes to Jesus and begs him to come to his home and heal his daughter, who is at the point of death. Jesus agrees but is slowed by the crowds and by his interaction with the woman above. By the time Jesus arrives at Jairus's house, the girl has died and the household is in mourning. Mark wrote that Jesus went to the little girl, "took her by the hand," and said, "Little girl . . . get up!" Immediately she gets up and begins to walk around (5:41–42). Once again, Jesus touches someone who shouldn't be touched, for according to the law, contact with a corpse was also considered nonkosher and demanded a period of quarantine and ritual washing.

In all three stories, the point isn't just that Jesus healed these people; the point is that Jesus *touched* these people. He embraced them just as he embraced other disparaged members of society, often regarded as "sinners" by the religious and political elite—prostitutes, tax collectors, Samaritans, Gentiles, the sick, the blind, and the deaf.

As Jeffrey John explained in *The Meaning in the Miracles*, these and other healing stories "seem to have been deliberately selected by the evangelists to show Jesus healing at least every category of persons who, according to the purity laws of Jesus' society, were specifically excluded and labeled unclean."[2]

"Each of these healings," he wrote, "is, of course, a demonstration of Jesus' healing power and compassion for the individual, but that is not the main point. Uppermost in the evangelist's mind—and far more relevant to us—is the miracle's universal significance: the overturning of social and religious barriers; the abolition of taboos; and Jesus' declaration of God's love and compassion for everyone, expressed in the systematic inclusion of each class of the previously excluded or marginalized."[3]

Many believe Jesus' miracles hold eschatological significance as well, which is just a fancy way of saying they reveal God's greatest dreams for the world, God's ultimate purpose for a wayward creation. The miracles of Jesus prefigure a future in which there is no more suffering, no more death, no more stigmatization, no more exclusion, no more chaos. They show us what it looks like for God's will to be done on earth as it is in heaven, and they invite us to buy into that future now, with every act of compassion and inclusion, every step toward healing and reconciliation and love.

"Hope," wrote N. T. Wright, "is what you get when you suddenly realize that a different worldview is possible, a worldview in which the rich, the powerful, and the unscrupulous do not after all have the last word. The same worldview shift that is demanded by the resurrection of Jesus is the shift that will enable us to change the world."[4]

The miracles of Jesus aren't magic tricks designed to awe prospective converts, nor are they tests from the past, meant to sort true believers from doubters. They are instructions, challenges. They show us what to do and how to hope.

The apostles certainly took this to heart as they spread word of the good news across the Roman Empire. In the book of Acts, Luke reported that with the aid of the Holy Spirit, the apostles themselves "performed many signs and wonders among the people," healing the sick, casting out demons, and raising the dead (5:12). They miraculously survived shipwrecks, snakebites, and angry mobs; God even sent an earthquake to break them out of jail. But perhaps most miraculous was the apostles' continued embrace of outsiders. One of the first Gentile converts to Christianity was a royal Ethiopian eunuch, whom Philip enthusiastically baptized and welcomed into the family of God even though eunuchs were sexual and ethnic minorities forbidden from worshipping in the temple (Acts 8:26–40). When Peter, a devout Jew, encountered the hospitality and faith of the Roman centurion Cornelius, he made the radical decision to not only meet with the Gentile, but to set aside nearly every kosher restriction in the Book and share a meal with him. "It is against our law for a Jew to associate with or visit a Gentile," Peter confesses to his new friend. "But God has shown me that I should not call anyone impure or unclean" (Acts 10:28).

The apostles remembered what many modern Christians tend to forget—that what makes the gospel offensive isn't who it keeps out but who it lets in.

So what does this mean for a perpetual skeptic like me, someone who isn't certain any of these miracles actually happened?

I like how Dallas Willard put it: "We don't believe something by merely saying we believe it," he said, "or even when we believe that we believe it. We believe something when we act as if it were true."[5]

So perhaps a better question than "Do I believe in miracles?" is "Am I acting like I do?" Am I including the people who are typically excluded? Am I feeding the hungry and caring for the sick? Am I holding the hands of the homeless and offering help to addicts? Am I working to break down religious and political barriers that marginalize ethnic, religious, and sexual minorities and people with disabilities? Am I behaving as though life is more than a meaningless, chaotic mess, that there is some order in the storm?

Activist Shane Claiborne likes to challenge Christians to not only believe in miracles but to "live in a way that might necessitate one."[6]

Indeed, the people in my life who seem most convinced of the reality of miracles are exactly the people who take the message of the Bible's miracles to heart: hospital chaplains, food pantry directors, addiction counselors, relief and development workers, nursing home volunteers, foster parents. These folks witness a whole lot of heartbreak from unmet needs and seemingly unanswered prayers, of course; they are neck-deep in it. But their proximity to the suffering and marginalized means they occasionally catch a glimpse of the miraculous—of limited rations multiplying like fishes and loaves, of centuries-long tribal suspicions melting away over a meal, of storms natural and man-made suddenly calmed by the presence of Jesus, of donations and care packages arriving at exactly the right time.

At least that's what they tell me.

I confess my own miracle stories are the sort for which I can readily offer alternative explanations (*Everyone thinks their child's birth is a miracle; what about the people who* didn't *narrowly avoid the accident?*), that my skeptical mind is both protecting me from exploitation and blinding me to a spectrum of colors I know others can see. A lot of religious folks think they can help by insisting over and over again how important it is to "just believe," as if belief were something one could conjure by force of will. But in my experience, simply *wanting* to believe doesn't work. The only thing that "works"—and probably only about half the time—is the long and storied spiritual discipline the sages of the faith refer to as "fake it till you make it."

Go to church.

Take communion.

Show up at the homeless shelter.

March in the protest.

Pray for healing.

Rebuke the chaos.

Act like you believe and maybe, at long last, you will. Move your feet and your heart will catch up.

It's been said that if you want to walk on water, you have to get out of the boat. Sometimes getting out of the boat looks like showing up for another recovery meeting. Sometimes it looks like filling out hospital paperwork for an elderly neighbor. Sometimes it looks like making a casserole for the family down with the flu or offering free babysitting for the friend with a job interview. Sometimes it looks like jumping when it matters.

"Jesus calls his disciples," wrote Sara Miles, "giving us authority to heal and sending us out. He doesn't show us how to reliably cure a molar pregnancy. He doesn't show us how to make a blind man see, dry every tear, or even drive out all kinds of demons. But he shows us how to enter into a way of life in which the broken and sick pieces are held in love, and given meaning. In which strangers literally touch each other, and in doing so make a community spacious enough for everyone."[7]

Not long after my exchange of fish stories with the priest at the dinner party, I found myself at yet another Episcopal church at yet another buffet table, this time asking the random strangers who had gathered about their *favorite* Bible stories.

"The one where Jesus meets his disciples on the beach," said a young mother, referring to a story from John's gospel.

Early one morning, shortly after Jesus has risen from the dead, the disciples are out fishing once again when they spot a mysterious figure on the shore.

"Friends, haven't you any fish?" the stranger asks (John 21:5).

When they answer no, he tells them to try casting on the other side of the boat. Sure enough, the net gets so heavy with fish, it nearly sinks the boat. The disciples immediately recognize the man as Jesus, and Peter is so overcome with emotion, he jumps out of the boat to swim to his teacher and friend. (Ol' Pete spends a lot of time jumping out of boats.) When the rest of the disciples catch up, lugging their catch behind them, they see Jesus has made a charcoal fire over which he is cooking some fish. He has bread too, and invites the disciples to join him for a meal. The text notes they catch a total of 153 fish, "and although there were so many, the net was not torn" (21:11 ESV).

"I like that one too," I said to the mother, and then posited the theory that the number 153 in rabbinic numerology signifies "completion" and perhaps corresponds to a specific prophecy in Ezekiel that describes a great river full of all kinds of fish flowing out of a restored temple. It's worth noting, I added, that John emphasized that the net was full but not torn, which means the net might symbolize the church, holding a great diversity of fish together in unity. Early Christian art depicts Peter and John holding a net on either side of a stream flowing from a temple, suggesting they made that connection too.

"Oh, I wasn't thinking about all that," the woman said with a smile. "I just like the idea of God frying up fish for breakfast."

THE LETTER

Give my greetings to the brothers and sisters at Laodicea, and to Nympha and the church in her house. After this letter has been read to you, see that it is also read in the church of the Laodiceans and that you in turn read the letter from Laodicea.

—Colossians 4:15–16

The sun has set over Laodicea, but Nympha's house glows with lamplight and hums with the comforting sounds of stifled laughter and hushed conversation. As soon as Aelia and Drucilla slip through the back door and into the crowded atrium together, they sense a stirring. There is news.

"What has happened?" Drucilla asks.

"Tychicus arrived from Colossae," whispers a young widow, "with a letter from Paul."[1]

At this, Aelia's heart leaps, for it means she gets to listen to

191

Nympha read. It mesmerizes her every time—the way Nympha enunciates every syllable carefully, gently, sometimes pausing to explain the meaning of the more difficult words or ideas, or to laugh forgivingly when one of the children throws a tantrum. Many at the gathering are women, slaves, and poor laborers, unable to read the letters from the apostles on their own, though a few are wealthy tradesmen, the owners of sprawling households. A passerby would find it strange to see them sitting together for a meal, master breaking bread with his slave, a wealthy patroness pouring wine for a poor prostitute. But this is what makes them different; this is what makes them Christians.

Nympha and her husband manufacture textiles, a lucrative trade in the Lycus Valley, renowned the world over for its purple cloth. They first heard the good news from a trader named Lydia, who brought it all the way from Thyatira, the story of an executed Jew who rose from the dead circulating like a strange new spice along the trade routes. While everyone in this household follows Jesus, Nympha usually manages the *ekklesia*, or gathering, herself. The community is known among the apostles as the church that meets at Nympha's house.

As the scent of fresh bread and stewed mullet wafts in from the kitchen, Aelia wonders for a moment if this is a short letter. She hasn't eaten all day. Her husband is a shepherd and poor, undoubtedly annoyed that a girl who came with such a small dowry would give him so much trouble over religion. He has been harsh with his mother lately too, for the government has made it illegal for widows to remain unmarried, but Drucilla insists on serving alongside the other widows in the church. This practice of caring for widows together, as a community, has proven especially controversial to the government, for it is believed that tampering with the household order is akin to tampering with the created universe. *Pax Romana* begins in the home, they always say, with obedient wives, slaves, and children.

And yet at these evening gatherings, Aelia has learned there should be no distinction between Jew and Gentile, male and female, slave and free, for all are one in Christ. Even the Scythians and barbarians are to be welcomed at the table. The degree to which followers of Jesus can accommodate Roman law without compromising their identity has thus become an issue of frequent debate at Nympha's house. Elsewhere, Christians have been imprisoned and even killed for resisting the empire, so the question lingering over every meal, every Scripture reading, and every prayer among the church at Laodicea is the same: *Do we risk our necks over differences with the government regarding class, commerce, worship, and household, or do we let things like that go?*

No one can seem to agree. Perhaps tonight's letter will help.

It is a beautiful letter, and tears run down Aelia's face as Paul, through Nympha, declares, "The gospel is bearing fruit and growing throughout the whole world—just as it has been doing among you since the day you heard it and truly understood God's grace."

Nympha's voice echoes strong and certain through the atrium, where at least thirty people sit on the tile floor. They hear about Paul's incarceration and persecution, about how Jesus is "the image of the invisible God, the firstborn over all creation," about guarding against false teachings and empty philosophy, about withholding judgment from those who hold different convictions regarding the observance of religious festivals and food, about how they should sing more hymns. Drucilla smiles wide at that last one. Aelia resolves to make peace with a sister with whom she has been in disagreement.

But then the mood shifts as Nympha reads—out loud!—that the church need not fear the government because Jesus "is the head over every power and authority." He has "disarmed the powers and

authorities," she reads, "and made a public spectacle of them, tri-
umphing over them by the cross."

A nervous murmur fills the room. What if someone overheard?
Those words could certainly be taken out of context by a passing
Roman soldier. This is an open-air atrium, for mercy's sake!

Nympha raises a hand to encourage calm.

"Notice the apostle says nothing of *overthrowing* the government," she says. "He speaks only of *exposing* it, *disarming* it."

"And yet he writes this letter from prison," a tradesman
grumbles to muffled snickers.

"What I understand the apostle to be saying," Nympha says, "is
that the crucifixion of Jesus exposed the empire, and all forms of
unjust authority, for what they are—cruel and empty, desperate and
weak. Rome executed an innocent man, for what? Healing the sick?
Telling stories? Riding a donkey into Jerusalem? The Messiah's obedience in humbling himself, loving his enemies, caring for the poor
and suffering, and turning away from violence made a mockery of
this opulent and oppressive empire. It made a mockery of religious
hypocrisy and exclusion. And his resurrection proves he is in fact
Lord and Master of all, for even Rome could not bury him, even
Caesar could not keep him dead for long."

The atrium echoes with shocked whispers. Nympha is a Roman
citizen, so these are dangerous words. Aelia notices for the first time
that the imperial mural that once adorned the atrium wall has been
painted over.

After a moment, Nympha reads on.

"Since, then, you have been raised with Christ, set your hearts
on things above, where Christ is, seated at the right hand of God. . . .
Do not lie to each other, since you have taken off your old self with
its practices and have put on the new self, which is being renewed
in knowledge in the image of its Creator. Here there is no Gentile

or Jew, circumcised or uncircumcised, barbarian, Scythian, slave or free, but Christ is all, and is in all.

"As God's chosen people, holy and dearly loved, clothe your-selves with compassion, kindness, humility, gentleness, and patience. Bear with each other and forgive one another if any of you has a grievance against someone. Forgive as the Lord forgave you. And over all these virtues put on love, which binds them all together in perfect unity."

Aelia rests her head on Drucilla's shoulder. She loves the imagery of dressing in compassion, kindness, and patience, and imagines slipping into love as though it were a purple robe, made of the best Colossian cloth. For a moment she forgets her hunger, forgets the dull dress and dirty fingernails that always seem so out of place in this fine home full of expensive silver. How could the apostle have known exactly what she needed to hear tonight, exactly how she felt?

"Wives submit yourselves to your husbands."

The words jolt Aelia from her reverie, not because they are for-eign, but because they are familiar.

In Rome, peasant and patron alike memorize the household codes at an early age, the most influential having been composed by Aristotle, who taught that the male head of house functions as a sovereign ruler over his wives, adult children, and slaves. Caesar believes a well-ordered state relies on well-ordered households, so perhaps the apostle means to encourage Christians to honor these long-held customs so as not to cause unnecessary offense.

Nympha clears her throat.

"Husbands love your wives."

This is different. None of the household codes Aelia knows speak of husbands loving their wives. While some wealthy couples marry for love, most marriages, like hers, are arranged, often when the girls are just children. The empire requires little from the male head of house besides allegiance to the state and control over his home, Aristotle's assertion that "the male is by nature better fitted to command than the female" an unquestioned assumption for centuries.

And yet, Aelia thinks, *in this house, Nympha holds authority.* Among Christians, many women do—Lydia, Junia, Priscilla, Phoebe. Paul refers to them as his coworkers and speaks of them as equals.

"Children, obey your parents in everything, for this pleases the Lord," Nympha continues. "Fathers, do not embitter your children, or they will become discouraged."

She pauses before getting to the next part. Every person in the room knows what comes next.

"Slaves obey your earthly masters in everything," Nympha reads. "Whatever you do, work at it with all your heart, as working for the Lord, not for human masters, since you know that you will receive an inheritance from the Lord. . . . It is the Lord Christ you are serving. Masters, provide your slaves with what is right and fair, because you know that you also have a Master in heaven."

At this the room erupts. Aelia is clearly not the only one puzzled. Slaves with an inheritance? Masters with a Master of their own? Some think the apostle is encouraging acquiescence to the empire. Others believe his words are subversive, and dangerously so.

"What does this mean for Onesimus?" someone shouts.

The room falls silent.

Onesimus was once the slave of a wealthy Christian named Philemon, a tradesman who hosts gatherings of Christians in his home in Colossae. Rumor has it Onesimus left the household under uncertain circumstances, befriended Paul in Rome, and now serves as something of an emissary on behalf of the apostles, delivering messages and arranging travel—with or without the blessing of his master. The question of what to do with slaves is a contentious one among the churches, for many of the Jews believe that when the Messiah announced in the synagogue that he came to liberate the poor and oppressed and "proclaim the year of the Lord's favor," he referred to the year of Jubilee, an ancient practice among their people in which, periodically, slaves were freed, debts forgiven, and land returned to original owners. This struck many of the Greek Christians as radically impractical and strange, a sure way to attract unwanted attention from the government.

Nympha seems reluctant to answer the question. She herself owns three slaves, all of whom sit in this very room. Her family boasts vast landholdings throughout the Lycus Valley, much of which they acquired when Rome seized the property of poor farmers who failed to pay their taxes. A year of Jubilee would not be in Nympha's best interest, to say the least.

She glances at Tychicus, who nods in encouragement.

"We have received word that Onesimus has returned to Colossae," she says, "with instructions from Paul that Philemon, and the rest of us, treat him as a brother, not a slave."

It's unclear how much of the letter is even heard after that. Several times Nympha's voice is drowned out by animated debate. Those who refrain from speaking seem lost in thought, unsure of what to do or say. Perhaps the apostle anticipated this, for the letter concludes with a reminder to "let your conversation be always full of grace, seasoned with salt."

Aelia thinks about this at the meal as she gobbles down the fish and bread, trying not to look too desperate or too much like a barbarian while stuffing a few extra dates and olives into her sack to bring home. She sits with Drucilla and the widows, who each have their own take on what has transpired.

"Just as we live in the empire, but are citizens of the kingdom of God, so we live in traditional households yet belong to the family of God," Drucilla ventures. "Maybe we are not called to overthrow the empire's social order, but to disarm it, to reveal its emptiness compared to gatherings like these where slave, master, husband, and wife are equals in service to Jesus."

An elderly widow jumps in.

"We can obey the empire's laws without following its rules."

"Exactly."

"And if husbands and wives love each other," another pipes in, "and slaves and masters respect one another, and if all submit to Jesus as the head of the Christian house, the 'chain of command' begins to break down."

"Indeed!"

Aelia wonders what Drucilla might have been had she been born into a family like Nympha's. The ekklesia has uncovered gifts of insight, wisdom, and leadership in her mother-in-law once obscured by lowly status and rural accent.

Later Nympha will read more letters, letters that speak of husbands loving their wives as Christ loves the church, willing to give their lives for them, and of Christians "submitting to one another" and living as "slaves to one another."

In Christian households across the region, the old chain of command begins to break down.

The night after the first letter, as Drucilla and Aelia slip quietly through the streets together, arm in arm on their way home, Drucilla wonders aloud if there will come a day when the world doesn't need household codes, when Jesus really is Lord and Master of every home.

That's when Aelia has a dangerous thought.

"They say *Pax Romana* begins in the home," she says. "Maybe revolution does too."

8

CHURCH STORIES

W hen you come, bring the cloak that I left with Carpus in Troas, and my scrolls, especially the parchments" (2 Timothy 4:13).

"I also baptized the household of Stephanas; beyond that, I don't remember if I baptized anyone else" (1 Corinthians 1:16).

"And one thing more: Prepare a guest room for me, because I hope to be restored to you in answer to your prayers" (Philemon 1:22).

It's a bit startling to encounter such personal, prosaic comments alongside some of Scripture's most memorable lines—"If I speak in the tongues of men or of angels, but do not have love, I am only a resounding gong or a clanging cymbal" (1 Corinthians 13:1); "Whatever is pure, whatever is lovely, whatever is admirable . . . think about such things" (Philippians 4:8). But the juxtaposition serves as a useful reminder that twenty-two of the New Testament's twenty-seven books aren't actually books. They're letters.

While literary epistles were common in the ancient world, the degree to which the genre dominated early Christian communication and instruction is striking. As New Testament scholar M.

Eugene Boring noted, "In no other religious community have letters become sacred Scripture or played such a formative role."[1]

Of course, the authors did not consider their letters Scripture at the time, nor did the recipients. The concerns of the world's first Christians were far more practical: how to get financial support for ministry, how to respond to arguments that Gentile converts needed to be circumcised, what to do with the influx of poor widows joining the church, which Roman laws to observe and which to challenge, and most important, how to foster theological and communal unity between Jews and Gentiles, rich and poor, men and women, new converts and mature Christians.

Although the Gospels appear before the Epistles in the ordering of the New Testament, it's likely the Epistles were written first, their messages revealing the most pressing questions, teachings, debates, and dramas of the early church. Most of these letters were composed by the apostle Paul, or by students writing in his name; others are attributed to the apostles Peter, James, Jude, and John.[2] The recipients were new followers of Jesus, most of them Gentiles, meeting in house churches in cities and towns across the Roman Empire.

Scholars generally divide ancient letters into two categories: "real letters" (correspondence intended for a specific and limited audience, like a soldier writing home), and "non-real letters" (literary works in epistolary form intended for the general public, like the published letters of the ancient philosopher Seneca). But the Epistles of the New Testament combine elements of both, and as a result, contain instructions both general—"In your relationships with one another, have the same mindset as Christ Jesus" (Philippians 2:5)—and specific—"Greet my dear friend Epenetus, who was the first convert to Christ in the province of Asia" (Romans 16:5). Furthermore, as letters emerging from an ancient Greco-Roman context, the Epistles presume certain cultural norms, like patriarchy, slavery, and patronage, and reflect the unique concerns of a minority religious sect in an imperial context. They expect women to wear head coverings (1 Corinthians 11:6), men to have short hair (11:14), and everyone to "greet one another with a holy kiss" (16:20). They wrestle with the age-old question of how to live as citizens of the kingdom of God in the shadow of the empire, as well as specific questions about whether Christians should buy discounted meat after it has been sacrificed to Roman gods. As a result, many passages carry a timeless, universal quality—"God is love" (1 John 4:16), while others reflect the unique challenges confronting followers of Jesus in the first century—"Eat anything sold in the meat market without raising questions of conscience" (1 Corinthians 10:25).

As Pastor Adam Hamilton explained, "When you read one of Paul's letters, or any other New Testament letter, you are reading someone else's mail. Christians often forget this. They read Paul's letters as though he wrote just for them. This works fine most of the time; Paul's instructions, his theological reflections and his practical concerns are amazingly timeless. But they become most meaningful, and we are least likely to misapply their teaching, when we seek to understand why he may have written this or that to a given church."[3]

A verse in a letter addressed to Titus illustrates this perfectly. Angered by some of the false teachings emerging from the island of Crete in the Mediterranean, which Titus is busy trying to fix, the apostle Paul declared, "One of Crete's own prophets has said it: 'Cretans are always liars, evil brutes, lazy gluttons.' This saying is true" (Titus 1:12–13).

Believe it or not, I've never once heard a sermon preached on this passage. And yet, if these words are truly the inerrant and unchanging words of God intended as universal commands for all people in all places at all times, and if the culture and context are irrelevant to the "plain meaning of the text," then apparently

Christians need to do a better job of mobilizing against the Cretan people. Perhaps we need to construct some "God Hates Cretans" signs, or lobby the government to deport Cretan immigrants, or boycott all movies starring Jennifer Aniston, whose father, I hear, is a lazy, evil, gluttonous Cretan.

I'm being facetious of course, but my point is, we dishonor the intent and purpose of the Epistles when we assume they were written in a vacuum for the purpose of filling our desk calendars with inspirational quotes or our theology papers with proof texts. (For the record, Paul told Titus to find among the Cretans leaders who were "blameless," "hospitable," "self-controlled," and "disciplined," so obviously he didn't apply the stereotype to *all* from the island.) The Epistles were never intended to be applied as law. Even conservative biblical scholar F. F. Bruce once remarked that the apostle Paul would "roll over in his grave if he knew we were turning his letters into torah."[4]

Like so much of Scripture, the Epistles were written *for* us but not *to* us. Modern readers benefit immensely from seeing how the earliest followers of Jesus applied his teachings to their lives and communities, particularly in the midst of outside persecution and internal debate. Just think of how much we owe the apostle Paul for reminding us "the fruit of the Spirit is love, joy, peace, patience, kindness, goodness, faithfulness, gentleness, [and] self control" and "against such things there is no law" (Galatians 5:22–23 NASB). That never stops being true. But we get into trouble when we mistake instructions intended for a specific group of people at a specific moment in history as universally binding for all.

We see this happen a lot with the New Testament household codes, found in various forms in Ephesians, Colossians, and 1 Peter. Many modern readers assume teachings about wives submitting to their husbands appear exclusively in the pages of Scripture and thus reflect uniquely "biblical" views about women's roles in the home. But to the people who first heard these letters read aloud in their churches, the words of Peter and Paul would have struck them as both familiar and strange, a sort of Christian remix on familiar Greco-Roman philosophy that positioned the male head of house as the rightful ruler over his subordinate wives, children, and slaves. By instructing men to love their wives and respect their slaves, and by telling everyone to "submit to one another" with Jesus as the ultimate head of house, the apostles offer correctives to cultural norms without upending them. They challenge new believers to reconsider their relationships with one another now that, in Christ, "there is neither Jew nor Gentile, neither slave nor free, nor is there male and female" (Galatians 3:28). The plot thickens when we pay attention to some of the recurring characters in the Epistles and see a progression toward more freedom and autonomy for slaves like Onesimus and women like Nympha, Priscilla, Junia, and Lydia.

So the question for modern readers, then, is whether the point of the New Testament household codes is to reinforce the Greco-Roman household structure as God's ideal for all people, in all places, for all time, or whether the point is to encourage Christians to imitate Jesus in their relationships, regardless of the culture or their status in it.

In a sense, the Epistles are a lot like wisdom literature, for they remind us that wisdom isn't just about knowing *what* is true; it's about knowing *when* it's true. Untangling culturally conditioned assumptions from universal truths in order to figure out how the wisdom of the Epistles might apply to us today is the task of modern-day hermeneutics, and it's not an easy one.

Consider, for example, the confusion around how ancient people understood the terms *natural* and *unnatural*. You'd never know it from current debate, but the Bible says very little about same-sex behavior and arguably nothing at all about committed same-sex relationships, whose prevalence in the ancient world is a subject of historical debate. One of the few, indirect references to same-sex activity in Scripture appears in Romans 1, where the apostle Paul, arguing that both Jews and Gentiles need salvation, alludes to Gentiles who were so "inflamed with lust" that the "women exchanged natural sexual relations for unnatural ones" and men "committed shameful acts with other men" (Romans 1:26–27).

It's important to understand that in the first century, same-sex relationships were not thought to be expressions of sexual orientations but rather products of excessive sexual desire wherein people engaging in same-sex behavior did so out of an excess of lust that could not be satisfied.[5] The most common forms of same-sex behavior in the Greco-Roman world were pederasty and sex between masters and their slaves, and the majority of men who indulged in those practices also engaged in heterosexual behavior with their wives. (In other words, they weren't, as we understand it today, *gay*.) In Paul's world, if a man took the active role in a sexual encounter, his behavior was deemed "natural," but if he took the passive role, his behavior was considered "unnatural," for he had taken the presumed position of a woman, deemed in that culture to be his inferior. The opposite was true for women: sexual passivity was deemed "natural," while dominance was "unnatural." These ideas were rooted in the honor-shame cultures of the Mediterranean and heavily influenced by patriarchal assumptions.

Now, lest you think this only applies to same-sex relationships, consider this: Paul uses the *very same language* in a letter to the Corinthian church to argue that women should wear head coverings and men shouldn't have long hair. "Judge for yourselves," he wrote, "Is it proper for a woman to pray to God with her head uncovered? Does not the very *nature* of things teach you that if a man has long hair, it is a *disgrace* to him, but if a woman has long hair, it is her glory?" (1 Corinthians 11:13–15, emphasis mine). He goes on to decry short-haired women and men with covered heads as similarly "unnatural," appealing to everything from the created order to male authority to the opinions of angels. "If anyone wants to be contentious about this," he concluded, "we have no other practice—nor do the churches of God" (11:16).

And yet many of the same Christians who condemn all same-sex behavior as "unnatural" according to the Bible, don't apply the same standards to head coverings or hair lengths among the men and women in their own congregations. Most understand Paul's language to the Corinthians to describe cultural customs, based on ancient views of gender roles, not universal truths.

So once again we are left with some questions: Must we adopt first-century, Mediterranean cultural assumptions about gender and sexuality in order to embrace the gospel Paul was preaching there? Must we condemn all short-haired women, long-haired men, and gay and lesbian couples as "unnatural"? Do we apply the same rightful condemnation of pederasty and rape in ancient Rome to loving, committed same-sex relationships today?

My experience loving and engaging with gay, lesbian, bisexual, and transgender friends has convinced me that the Bible has been unfairly used against them, often with tragic results, but Christians can disagree on that. And they often do, fiercely.

With all these cultural angles to consider and heated debates to navigate, a lot of folks lose faith in the Epistles. They assume that Paul was just a first-century misogynist, the churches of Rome, Ephesus, Corinth, and Colossae merely products of their time, just as divisive and dysfunctional as churches today. There have been moments when I too have grown weary of confronting prejudices advanced in the Bible's name and, frustrated, found myself wondering, *Why letters? Why would God use a medium so easily misunderstood and misapplied to introduce the gospel to the world?*

Dr. Boring addressed the question brilliantly. "The early Christians did not believe that God became incarnate in humanity in general," he wrote, "or in some abstract principle, but in one particular Aramaic-speaking Jew, born in an obscure land under Roman rule, crucified under the local governor Pontius Pilate."

This "scandal of particularity," he said, "is related to the essential character of human life. No one lives in general; every human life is unique. The letters of the New Testament are appropriate to the incarnation."[6]

No one lives in general—not even Christ or his church. The Christian life isn't about intellectual assent to a set of propositions, but about following Jesus in the context of actual marriages, actual communities, actual churches, actual political differences, actual budget meetings, actual cultural changes, actual racial tensions, actual theological disagreements. Like it or not, you can't be a Christian on your own. Following Jesus is a group activity, and from the beginning, it's been a messy one; it's been an incarnated one. The reason the Bible includes so many seemingly irrelevant details about donkeys falling into pits and women covering their heads and Cretans being liars and Jews and Gentiles sharing meals together is because, believe it or not, God cares about that stuff—because God cares about us.

No doubt when the Christians of 2218 read our books, blog posts, and church newsletters, they will think to themselves, *Why in the world was that an issue of debate?* and *Can you believe that's how they thought about things back then?* and *How was it not obvious that LEGGINGS ARE NOT PANTS?* Yet the Spirit will be just as present and active then as it is now, as it was more than two thousand years ago.

While the nature of our differences and debates has changed, the apostles' advice about how to handle those conflicts remains applicable to us all.

"Be kind and compassionate to one another, forgiving each other, just as in Christ God forgave you" (Ephesians 4:32).

"Accept the one whose faith is weak, without quarreling over disputable matters. One person's faith allows them to eat anything, but another . . . eats only vegetables. The one who eats everything must not treat with contempt the one who does not, and the one who does not eat everything must not judge the one who does. . . . Do not destroy the work of God for the sake of food" (Romans 14:1–3, 20).

"You are the body of Christ, and each one of you is a part of it. . . . The eye cannot say to the hand, 'I don't need you!' And the head cannot say to the feet, 'I don't need you!' . . . If one part suffers, every part suffers with it; if one part is honored, every part rejoices with it" (1 Corinthians 12:27, 21, 26).

"Do not let the sun go down while you are still angry" (Ephesians 4:26).

The Epistles reveal, with startling concreteness, how the announcement of God's victory over sin and death through Jesus played itself out in real life among a group of highly dissimilar people.

"The Bible looks the way it does," wrote Peter Enns, "because, like Jesus, when God shows up, it's in the thick of things."[7]

〜

Even after I'd come to terms with the Bible's war stories and learned to embrace the Bible's tensions and contradictions as fitting and good, even after I'd given up on trying to force the Bible to be something it's not and resolved to keep wrestling with the confounding force that it is, there remained one obstacle in the way of a fresh start with my once beloved Magic Book. To make peace with the Bible, I had to make peace with Paul.

I know I'm not the only woman who has been crowded into a corner after a church service or Christian conference by a red-faced man insisting I shouldn't be allowed to speak there because the Bible is *clear:* "I do not permit a woman to teach or to assume authority over a man; she must be quiet" (1 Timothy 2:12).

I once held the quivering body of a middle-aged woman, sobbing with her head on my shoulder, as she told me her story of living with an abusive husband for twenty years, her family and church insisting she remain with him because the Bible is *clear:* "Wives submit to your husbands."

For many of my gay, lesbian, bisexual, and transgender friends, what they know of Paul they know from verses scribbled across protest signs held by people who insist that God hates the likes of them. For those who grew up in church, what they remember most—what haunted them through countless sleepless nights and thoughts of suicide—was the fear that if they came out, they would go to hell, because the Bible is *clear:* "Neither the sexually immoral nor idolaters nor adulterers nor men who have sex with men . . . will inherit the kingdom of God" (1 Corinthians 6:9–10).

In the buildup to the American Civil War, Christian ministers wrote nearly half of all defenses of slavery, often citing Scripture in support of the Confederate cause. The Southern Baptist denomination exists today because Baptists from the South did not want to be told by Baptists in the North that owning black people was wrong. After all, they argued, the Bible is *clear:* "Slaves obey your earthly masters" (Ephesians 6:5).

Ask someone involved in the civil rights movement of the fifties and sixties and they'll tell you their acts of civil disobedience—staging sit-ins at "whites only" restaurants, marching across that bridge in Selma—were often met with objections from white Christians who claimed such actions were "unbiblical," because the Bible is *clear*: "Let everyone be subject to the governing authorities" (Romans 13:1).

The supposed clarity of Scripture, and specifically of the apostle Paul, has been invoked far too often in far too many cruelties to remain unaddressed. For many progressive believers, Christianity's most famous missionary is something of a thorn in their flesh (see what I did there?), Paul's words about women, sex, slavery, the death penalty, and submitting to the government invoked so routinely in opposition to their social causes that they've grown exasperated by him. On the other hand, among more conservative believers, Paul gets the opposite treatment and tends to be idolized for his theological lucidity on matters of salvation, justification, election, and atonement. I once heard an evangelical pastor brag that he had never preached from any biblical text that wasn't authored by Paul, not even the Gospels. I couldn't help but laugh when the same guy gave Catholics a hard time for venerating Mary.

Both groups, I suspect, suffer from the habit of dislocating Paul from his original context and mission. N. T. Wright insisted that the New Testament "must be read so that the stories, and the Story, which it tells can be heard *as* stories, not as rambling ways of declaring unstoried 'ideas.'"[8] When we unmoor the Epistles from their larger story, we tend to think of Paul as a disembodied voice affirming or unsettling our own points of view, rather than a religious, first-century Jew whose life was upended by an encounter with Jesus Christ.

As it turns out, the letters of Paul weren't written by a crotchety misogynist intent on regulating the behaviors of women and minorities for millennia to come, nor were they composed by a godlike philosopher disseminating soteriological truths into the universe from an ivory tower. The apostle Paul was a smart, worldly, and broad-minded Jew who had been utterly transformed by what he saw as his singular mission in life: to preach the gospel of Jesus Christ to the Gentiles and welcome them in to Israel's story. In pursuit of that mission, Paul was determined to break down every religious, ethnic, and cultural barrier that stood in the way.

(Here it's worth noting that in the ancient world, letters were sometimes composed in the name of a famous teacher from the past, and scholars suspect that, given the language employed and other historical indicators, Ephesians, 1 and 2 Timothy, and Titus were not composed by Paul himself, but by students writing under his name. Seven epistles remain largely undisputed as authentically Pauline—Romans, 1 and 2 Corinthians, Galatians, Philippians, 1 Thessalonians, Philemon—while Colossians and 2 Thessalonians are debatable.[9] For simplicity, I refer to Paul as the author of all the epistles attributed to him.)

Paul of Tarsus was a proud Jew, "circumcised on the eighth day, of the people of Israel, of the tribe of Benjamin, a Hebrew of Hebrews" (Philippians 3:5). A Pharisee and the son of a Pharisee, he knew and loved the Torah and maintained his Jewish identity in a pagan culture. He was also a Roman citizen and Greek, profoundly influenced by Hellenistic thought. Paul knew at least three languages—Greek, Hebrew, and Aramaic—and himself possessed both a Jewish name, *Saul,* and a Greek and Roman name, *Paul.*

Originally a persecutor of Christians, Paul experienced a dramatic conversion on the road to Damascus one day, when a blinding light threw him to the ground and a voice from heaven asked, "Saul, Saul, why do you persecute me?" (Acts 9:4). Despite their fears, the Christians in Damascus and Jerusalem welcomed Paul into their homes and cared for him until his sight was restored, acts of radical, risky hospitality that undoubtedly shaped Paul's posture toward others in the years to come. As he came to terms with this divine interruption to his own story, Paul began to understand its place in a larger story, and to preach Jesus as the long-awaited Messiah, whose life, death, and resurrection fulfilled biblical prophecy, in particular Isaiah's vision that Israel would be "a light for the Gentiles" that would bring "salvation to the ends of the earth" (Isaiah 49:6; Acts 13:47).

This message of good news for *all* people of *all* nations became Paul's obsession. As he traveled the region with other followers of Jesus, sharing the gospel in cities across Asia and Europe, he almost always preached first to the Jews in the synagogues and then to the Gentiles at their marketplaces, academic forums, and homes. He described himself as a "slave to everyone" willing to become "all things to all people . . . for the sake of the gospel" (1 Corinthians 9:19, 22, 23).

As author and biblical scholar Stephen J. Binz explained, Paul "used his global, multicultural, and breadth of thought for the sake of the universal gospel he proclaimed. Paul was a man who could talk with rabbis on the streets of Jerusalem and with philosophers on the streets of Athens . . . He knew the ancient wisdom of the Hebrew Scriptures, and he knew the wisdom of Greek literature, such as that of Homer, Sophocles, and Plato."[10]

Paul typically had more success with the Gentiles than the Jews, though he routinely faced angry mobs from both camps. He once triggered a riot in Ephesus when his work threatened to put a dent in the sale of tchotchkes devoted to the goddess Artemis, whose temple drew tourists to the town. Unsurprisingly, Paul's declaration of the good news found special resonance among people of lower classes, and with slaves, widows, and women.

In fact, women proved to be a vital force in the ministry of Paul, serving as apostles, teachers, benefactors, and friends. Paul was once imprisoned with a woman named Junia, whom he described as "outstanding among the apostles" (Romans 16:7), and some of his dearest friends were Priscilla and Aquila, a pair I like to think of as the church's first power couple, complete with rhyming monikers— *Prisquila*, if you like—whom Paul appears to have regarded as equals, sometimes referring first to Priscilla and sometimes referring first to Aquila. Priscilla was a renowned teacher whose mentorship of Apollos helped correct some of the famous preacher's early views. In Paul's letter to the Romans, he thanked multiple women for their leadership and support, referring to them as his "co-workers." Romans 16 includes thanks to Junia and Priscilla, as well as a deacon named Phoebe, a "dear friend" named Persis, and Mary, Tryphena, Tryphosa, and a host of other women "who worked very hard in the Lord" (v. 12). The degree to which Paul reinforced traditional gender roles in his letters varies from church to church and city to city. In places where women in leadership assisted in the spreading of the gospel, Paul encouraged it; where it might prove too disruptive or confusing, he discouraged it. (Notably, the most restrictive New Testament instructions regarding women in leadership appear in a letter to Timothy in Ephesus, home of the infamous Artemis riots.) In fact, in his first-century context, Paul would likely have been perceived as radically inclusive and egalitarian. For him, nothing mattered more than *unleashing* the gospel and moving out of the way any unnecessary cultural or religious obstructions that might impede its proliferation.

We see this attitude in the position he took in one of the first big debates of the early church. As Gentiles began responding to the gospel and believing in Jesus as Savior, some Jewish Christians understandably assumed that these new converts ought to receive the sign of circumcision, follow Jewish dietary restrictions, and observe other precepts of the law before becoming part of the community of

God's people. If Gentiles wanted in on the blessings of the covenant, they must be faithful to the Torah. That only seemed "biblical."

But Paul and his friend Barnabas vehemently disagreed, so much so that they traveled back to Jerusalem to try and settle the dispute with the apostles and elders there. At this Jerusalem Council, the pair joined Peter, James, and other apostolic heavyweights to hash it all out, and in one of the most significant religious decisions in history, it was determined that Gentiles did not need to be circumcised but should only abstain from those foods and activities that might impede their ability to share a table of fellowship and live in harmony with their Jewish brothers and sisters.

"It is my judgment," the apostle James concluded, ". . . that we should not make it difficult for the Gentiles who are turning to God" (Acts 15:19).

Of course, many remained unconvinced, which is why Paul spent so much time in his letters arguing for grace over law. He wasn't speaking in some abstract way against religious legalism or "salvation by works," nor was he damning the entire Jewish community of which he was still proudly a part. He was simply making the same case he had been making from the beginning, that Jews and Gentiles are now one in the family of God because the faithfulness of Jesus on behalf of Israel and for the rest of the world "made the two groups one and has destroyed the barrier, the dividing wall of hostility" (Ephesians 2:14). Perhaps the most powerful reinforcement of this commitment appears in Paul's trademark greeting, completely unique in ancient literature. Every New Testament letter authored by Paul or in his name begins with "grace and peace to you," a combination of the Greek word *charis* (grace) with the Hebrew word *shalom* (peace), a seemingly mundane turn of phrase packed with rich theological meaning for both groups, pointing them toward mercy, wholeness, justice, and unity.

Yes, Paul did a lot of theologizing. The man never met a metaphor he didn't like. But every letter he wrote was in service to an inclusive, grace-filled gospel that he believed was good news for everyone, Jew and Gentile, rich and poor, man and woman alike.

So in considering the writings of Paul, the question is not, *Are head coverings good or bad?* The question is, in that context, *Did head coverings help or hurt the advancement of the gospel and the preservation of unity?*

The question is not, *Should Christians eat meat?* but rather, in that context, *Did eating meat help or hurt the advancement of the gospel and the preservation of unity?* And as we consider the application of Paul's teachings in our various contexts today, the question is not, *Should women be allowed to preach?* but *Do women preachers help or hurt the advancement of the gospel and the preservation of unity?* Paul was smart enough to know the answers to these questions would vary from church to church and person to person, so surely he was smart enough to also know they would vary from culture to culture and century to century.

Was Paul a man of his time? Of course. But that's exactly the point. God meets us where we are, as we are. The Spirit shows up in the thick of it.

We don't have to embrace everything about Paul's culture in order to embrace the good news he preached within it, that "neither death nor life nor angels nor rulers nor things present nor things to come nor powers nor height nor depth nor anything else in all creation, will be able to separate us from the love of God in Christ Jesus our Lord" (Romans 8:38–39 ESV).

EPILOGUE

"AND THEN . . ."

My sister-in-law, Maki, has the kind of laugh that will carry a mile. You hear it booming from her large Atlanta-area kitchen, where a gaggle of friends, family, and neighbors always gather, snacking on appetizers and sharing stories as Maki shouts above the sizzle of some savory masterpiece brewing in her frying pan. If you come for a visit, you will stay; there's no sense in leaving your shoes on. When friends from the Philippines are in town, Maki oscillates between languages with seamless ease, as conversant in Filipino politics as she is on the new iPhone, Christian theology, and the latest dustup on reality TV. Gregarious, entrepreneurial, and whip-smart, Maki is the only person on the planet to successfully convince me to try karaoke. She has a way of coaxing the Beyoncé out of even the stodgiest introvert.

She's also the best listener I've ever met. I've watched in wonder as otherwise standoffish family members divulged their innermost feelings over chicken *tapa* and rice, as the shiest neighbor on the block suddenly commanded the attention of a room with a hilarious tale of a blind date gone wrong. With Maki's encouragement, the most mundane recounting of your day at work will blossom into a tale of intrigue and surprise, all thanks to the magic she gives two little words:

"And then."

Make an offhand comment about getting stuck in traffic on the way over, and Maki will reply, *"And then?"*

Tell her you sat for half an hour next to a guy in a station wagon who was clearly listening to the same radio station as you.

"And then, and then?"

Commence with a dramatic impression of the flamboyant driver and his impassioned lip sync of Adele's "Hello," which only drew a chuckle from you at the time, but which now has a room of twenty Filipinos laughing hysterically, as Maki continues to urge, *"And then? And then? And then?"*

Everyone knows and loves Maki by what has become her signature linguistic tick. I suppose this is why you always leave her house feeling both fuller and lighter.

I only recently learned that my sister-in-law is employing what Hebrew scholars term the *waw consecutive,* an element of syntax upon which Hebrew stories are built. By prefixing a verb form with the letter *waw* in order to change tense, the writers of Hebrew Scripture move a story along by essentially saying, *"And then, and then, and then."*

"The composers of biblical prose," wrote author and scholar Gregory Mobley, "appended the simplest conjunction, 'and,' to a line, gave it a little extra vocalization . . . doubled the initial consonant of the word to which the 'and' was attached, and *voila:* the Biblical Hebrew 'and then.' 'There was light *and then* God saw that the light was good *and then* there was evening *and then* there was morning, and *then and then and then,*' before you know it, you are standing with Moses on Mount Nebo at the end of Deuteronomy, light-years from when God first peered over the abyss."[1]

Not only do the Bible's "and thens" work within particular narratives to move from one event to the next, but they also work to move along the larger narrative. Genesis *and then* Exodus. Abraham *and then* Isaac. Israel *and then* Jesus.

Christians believe we live in the "and then" after Jesus' resurrection and before his return. We live inside an unfinished story, a story that began with the Spirit of God hovering over the primordial waters at the beginning of time and which took a dramatic, climactic turn two thousand years ago when that same God became human, lived among us, and beat death once and for all. We share this story with Mary Magdalene and the apostle Paul. We share it with Saint Augustine and Julian of Norwich, Desmond Tutu and Leymah Gbowee. We share it with the pastor who runs the soup kitchen out of the church basement and with the first guy in line to eat there each week. The stories we tell with our lives, then, aren't meaningless absurdities, tragic in their brevity, but rather subplots of a grander narrative, every moment charged with significance, as we contribute our own riffs, soliloquies, and plot twists to the larger epic, the Holy Spirit coaxing us along with an ever-ebullient, *And then? And then? And then?*

In explaining the significance of the resurrection, N. T. Wright put it like this:

> What you do in the Lord is not in vain. You are not oiling the wheels of a machine that's about to roll over a cliff. You are not restoring a great painting that's shortly going to be thrown on the fire. You are not planting roses in a garden that's about to be dug up for a building site. You are—strange though it may seem, almost as hard to believe as the resurrection itself—accomplishing

something that will become in due course part of God's new world. Every act of love, gratitude, and kindness every work of art or music inspired by the love of God and delight in the beauty of his creation; every minute spent teaching a severely handicapped child to read or to walk; every act of care and nurture, of comfort and support, for one's fellow human beings and for that matter one's fellow nonhuman creatures; and of course every prayer, all Spirit-led teaching, every deed that spreads the gospel, builds up the church, embraces and embodies holiness rather than corruption, and makes the name of Jesus honored in the world—all of this will find its way, through the resurrecting power of God, into the new creation that God will one day make.[2]

Imagine if you believed this. Imagine if every day you behaved as though this were true.

"The task of theology," wrote Mobley, "is the linking of our individual story to the biggest story we can imagine."[3]

If the biggest story we can imagine is about God's loving and redemptive work in the world, then our lives will be shaped by that epic. If the biggest story we can imagine is something else, like religious nationalism, or "follow your bliss," or "he who dies with the most toys wins," then our lives will be shaped by those narratives instead.

This is why it's so important to tell our children good stories. Dan and I are often asked how we plan to introduce the Bible to our son, and I generally avoid answering that question in much detail because, so far, parenting is one big exercise in changing plans. But we certainly don't intend to keep the Bible's stories from him. I want my son to be exposed to a wide variety of stories, including, when he's ready, strange and scary ones, *not because they tell us that dragons exist, but because they tell us that dragons can be defeated.* So I suspect that, with the Bible, we will start with the parables of Jesus and perhaps some well-behaved psalms, then move on to Adam and Eve, Jonah and the big fish, Jericho, the manger, and the cross. Sure, he'll get the edited versions at first, just like we did, and of course he'll pick up all sorts of strange interpretations from his friends, the culture, and theologically questionable cartoon adaptations; there's really no avoiding that. But I hope that by teaching him first to simply love these stories as they are, to relish their strange appeal, he will remember their magic when he rediscovers them in his own way someday.

Researchers tell us one of the greatest gifts we can give our children is the ability to tell stories. Helping them apply narrative to their everyday experiences, and to see a purpose and direction in the forces that shape their lives, improves both cognitive function and well-being. Recounting everything from a skinned knee to a school field trip to a traumatic event like a car accident or death in the family with the aid of storytelling helps children make sense of their fears and emotions and manage them in a healthy way.

"The drive to understand why things happen to us is so strong that the brain will continue to try making sense of an experience until it succeeds," wrote Daniel Siegel and Tina Payne Bryson in *The Whole-Brain Child*. "As parents, we can help this process along through storytelling."[4]

Our little boy is not even two years old, and already I've practiced this sort of storytelling with him. At present the stories are high in drama and low in complexity—*"You were enjoying your monkey stick, but then you ran with it and fell on it, huh? And that hurt, didn't it?"* (Please don't ask me what a monkey stick is.) But as time goes on, they will no doubt evolve into more complicated tales about sharing toys, taking turns, sticking with it, and being kind. At some point we will tell him the story of how his parents met—in

Dr. Jim Coffield's Psych 101 class at Bryan College in 1999—and how I shocked his father by calling him a Yankee. We will tell him the story of his birth on Candlemas Day, the story of his hometown and the famous Scopes Monkey Trial, the story of Uncle Wick and Aunt Toots. We will tell him about Jesus.

But we haven't got there yet. Presently, our son's curiosity about the world presents as a singular and insatiable compulsion to properly identify *all of the things*, a compulsion he expresses by dramatically extending his arm, pointing his finger at some unsuspecting person or plant or household appliance, and shouting with breathless insistence, "a-DA?"

What's that?

"a-DA?"

"That's an elephant, buddy."

"a-DA?"

"An elephant."

"a-DA?"

"It's the little stuffed elephant your grandma gave you."

"a-DA?"

"I SAID IT'S AN ELEPHANT, LIKE THE ANIMAL AT THE ZOO!"

" a-DA?"

Parents of young children will no doubt be familiar with those long years when it seems not a moment goes by without someone incessantly quizzing you with "Why?" "How come?" or "What's that?" often forcing an awkward confrontation with your own ignorance—*Gosh, why is the sky blue?* I've often said that those who say having a childlike faith means not asking questions haven't met too many children.

Psychologists say the best way to handle children at this stage of development is not to answer their questions directly but instead to tell them a story. As pediatrician Alan Greene explained, "After conversing with thousands of children, I've decided that what they really mean is, 'That's interesting to me. Let's talk about that together. Tell me more, please?'"[5]

Questions are a child's way of expressing love and trust. They are a child's way of starting a conversation. So instead of simply insisting over and over again that the object of my son's attention is, in fact, an elephant, I might tell him about how, in India, elephants are symbols of good luck, or about how some say elephants have the best memories of all the animals. I might tell him about the time I saw an elephant spin a basketball on the tip of his trunk, or about how once there was an elephant named Horton who heard a Who. I might tell him that once upon a time, there was an elephant and four blind men; each man felt a different part of the elephant's body: the ears, the tail, the side, and the tusk . . .

Sometimes, as I'm doing this, my son will crawl into my lap, put his head on my chest, and just listen to the story, his questions quieted, his body relaxed. And I realize this is all he wanted to begin with—to be near me, to hear the familiar cadence of my voice, to know he's safe and not alone.

We grown-ups aren't so different. We scurry around the world, grabbing bits of theology here and pieces of philosophy there, Bibles tucked under our arms as we point frantically at every question and every mystery that befalls us, asking, "*a-DA? a-DA? a-DA? What's that? What's that? What's that?*"

We may wish for answers, but God rarely give us answers. Instead, God gathers us up into soft, familiar arms and says, "Let me tell you a story."

ACKNOWLEDGMENTS

It was in the midst of writing this book that I became a mother, the corners of my world both expanding to encompass reaches of love previously unknown and contracting to attend to the daily tasks of waking, nursing, diapering, laundering. Every book takes a village, but this one took a veritable city of friends, family, agents, and editors willing to give of their time and to work at odd hours to ensure I could continue writing.

I am most grateful to my husband, Dan, who rose to the occasion of fatherhood with all the joy and tenderness I expected but with more perseverance than I thought possible. Every extra hour at the park, every middle-of-the-night bottle-feeding, every stroller ride around and around the living room made it possible for me to sneak in a hundred words here and a thousand words there, to finish this project the way I wanted to finish it. Even on the hardest of days, I am so grateful to be part of a partnership like this one.

I dedicated this book to my mother-in-law, Norma Evans, whose generosity of spirit has touched many lives over the years, including my own. Some people just know how to *help*. Large portions of this work were composed while she happily folded our laundry and washed our dishes and sang our baby boy to sleep. Few people better embody the biblical admonitions to welcome the stranger, care for the orphan and widow, and give without expecting anything in return. There is no doubt in my mind that Norma Evans has entertained more than her fair share of "angels unawares" (Hebrews 13:2 KJV).

I've never been more grateful to be close to my parents, both relationally and geographically. Over the course of the last two years, Peter and Robin Held tirelessly brought food, listened to me cry, and offered free therapy and babysitting. My sister, Amanda, and brother-in-law, Tim, remained steadfast in their support—two of the best cheerleaders I know.

The team at Thomas Nelson has once again been thoughtful, creative, and above all, *patient*. Thanks to Jenny Baumgartner for challenging me with some of the wisest and sharpest edits I've ever received, and to Joey Paul for offering early notes that dramatically improved the tone and emphasis of the book. Jared Byas and Nyasha Junior provided excellent scholarly reviews, and Janene MacIvor and Jenn McNeil, thorough and thoughtful copyedits. On more than one occasion, my friend Peter Enns willingly answered random questions about the Old Testament via 2:00 a.m. e-mails. In addition, I'm grateful for Stephanie Tresner, whom I consider the best in the business when it comes to online marketing, reader engagement, and appropriate .gif sending. Thanks, too, to Brian Hampton for once again taking me on.

I'm grateful, as always, to my literary agent, Rachelle Gardner, and my booking agent, Jim Chaffee, both of whom prioritize my well-being over my productivity. My readers, too, have proven exceedingly patient and kind.

Thanks to the Episcopal Church, specifically Saint Luke's Episcopal Church in Cleveland, Tennessee, and the Episcopal

ACKNOWLEDGMENTS

Diocese of East Tennessee, for so warmly welcoming me and my family into your community, and Bishop Shannon Sherwood Johnson and the Diocese of Virginia for offering such valuable encouragement and feedback when this project was just getting off the ground.

Finally, I am thankful to Henry for unlocking in me stores of love I didn't even know I had, for filling this house with so much laughter and music, for making it impossible to stay cynical in a year of social and political upheaval. There is not a writer in the world who could adequately capture the love I have for you, sweet boy. May you always know without a doubt that you are loved, and may you always be surrounded by good stories.

ABOUT THE AUTHOR

Rachel Held Evans is a *New York Times* bestselling author who writes about faith, doubt, and life in the Bible Belt. Rachel has been featured in the *Washington Post, The Guardian, Christianity Today, Slate,* the *Huffington Post,* and the *CNN Belief Blog,* and on NPR, BBC, *Today,* and *The View.* She served on President Obama's Advisory Council on Faith-Based and Neighborhood Partnerships, and keeps a busy schedule speaking at churches, conferences, and college and universities around the country. Rachel is married to Dan and they have two young children. A lifelong Alabama Crimson Tide fan, Rachel's preferred writing fuel is animal crackers and red wine.

NOTES

INTRODUCTION

1. Addie Zierman, "Recovering from Legalism: Dear Addie #7," Off the Page, June 29, 2016, https://offthepage.com/2016/06/29/recovering-from-legalism-dear-addie-7/.
2. Peter Enns, *The Bible Tells Me So* (New York: HarperOne, 2014), 9.
3. Burton L. Visotzky, *Reading the Book* (Philadelphia: Jewish Publication Society, 2005), 18.
4. N. T. Wright, "How Can the Bible Be Authoritative?" NTWrightPage, July 12, 2016, http://ntwrightpage.com/2016/07/12/how-can-the-bible-be-authoritative/.
5. Neil Gaiman, *Coraline* (New York: HarperCollins, 2012), ix.

THE TEMPLE

1. Background for this chapter is drawn from John Walton, *The Lost World of Genesis One* (Downers Grove, IL: InterVarsity Press, 2009), and from Ilan Ben Zion, "'By the Rivers of Babylon' Exhibit Breathes Life into Judean Exile," *The Times of Israel*, February 1, 2015, http://www.timesofisrael.com/by-the-rivers-of-babylon-exhibit-breathes-life-into-judean-exile/.
2. Isaiah 66:1–2, author's paraphrase.

CHAPTER 1: ORIGIN STORIES

1. Peter Enns, "Understanding Adam," BioLogos Foundation (scholar essays), accessed February 5, 2018, https://biologos.org/uploads /projects/enns_adam_white_paper.pdf.
2. Peter Enns, *Inspiration and Incarnation* (Grand Rapids: Baker Academic, 2005), 55.
3. Daniel Taylor, *Tell Me a Story: The Life-Shaping Power of Our Stories* (St. Paul: Bog Walk Press, 2001).
4. James Cone, *God of the Oppressed* (Maryknoll, NY: Orbis Books, 2003), 93.
5. Monica Coleman, *Bipolar Faith: A Black Woman's Journey with Depression and Faith* (Minneapolis: Fortress Press, 2016), xvii–xviii.
6. Coleman, xix.
7. Coleman, 342.
8. Joan Didion, *The White Album* (New York: Simon & Schuster, 1979), 11.
9. Barbara Hardy, "Toward a Poetics of Fiction: An Approach Through Narrative," *Novel* 2 (1968): 5.
10. Wilda Gafney, *Womanist Midrash: A Reintroduction to the Women of the Torah and the Throne* (Louisville: Westminster John Knox Press, 2017), 4–5.
11. Timothy Beal, *The Rise and Fall of the Bible* (Boston: Mariner Books, 2012), 188.
12. Visotzky, *Reading the Book*, 56.
13. Peter Enns and Jared Byas, *Genesis for Normal People* (Englewood, CO: Patheos Press, 2012), 91.
14. Madeleine L'Engle, *A Stone for a Pillow: Journeys with Jacob* (New York: Convergent, 2017), 165.

THE WELL

1. Background for this chapter is drawn from Genesis 16 and Delores Williams, *Sisters in the Wilderness: The Challenge of Womanist God-Talk* (Maryknoll, NY: Orbis Books, 1993).

CHAPTER 2: DELIVERANCE STORIES

1. Allen Dwight Callahan, *The Talking Book: African Americans and the Bible* (New Haven, CT: Yale University Press, 2008), 40.

2. Callahan, xiv.

3. Avot 5:22.

4. Broderick Greer, "Theology as Survival," January 7, 2016, *Broderick Greer* (blog), http://www.broderickgreer.com/blog/survivaltheology.

5. Lauren Winner, *Still: Notes on a Mid-Faith Crisis* (New York: HarperOne, 2013), 135.

6. Winner, 136.

7. Walter Brueggemann, *The Land: Place as Gift, Promise, and Challenge in Biblical Faith* (Minneapolis: Fortress Press, 2002), 39.

8. Jonathan Martin, *Prototype* (Carol Stream, IL: Tyndale, 2013), 50, 65.

9. Douglas A. Knight and Amy-Jill Levine, *The Meaning of the Bible: What the Jewish Scriptures and the Christian Old Testament Can Teach Us* (New York: HarperOne, 2013), 103.

10. Walter Brueggemann, *The Creative Word: Canon as a Model for Biblical Education* (Minneapolis: Fortress Press, 2015), 31.

11. Elton Trueblood, cited in Brian McLaren, *A New Kind of Christianity* (New York: HarperCollins, 2010), 114.

CHAPTER 3: WAR STORIES

1. William P. Trent and Benjamin W. Wells, eds., *Colonial Prose and Poetry: The Transplanting of Culture* (New York: Thomas Y. Crowell, 1901), 139.

2. Phyllis Trible, *Texts of Terror: Literary-Feminist Readings of Biblical Narratives* (Philadelphia: Fortress Press, 1984), 2.

3. John Piper, "What Made It Okay for God to Kill Women and Children in the Old Testament?" *Desiring God* (blog), February 27, 2010, http://www.desiringgod.org/interviews/what-made-it-ok-for-god-to-kill-women-and-children-in-the-old-testament.

4. Brené Brown, *The Gifts of Imperfection: Let Go of Who You Think You're Supposed to Be and Embrace Who You Are* (Center City, MN: Hazelden, 2010), 70.

5. Thomas Paine, *The Works of Thomas Paine*, ed. Moncure Daniel Conway (Frankston, TX: TGS, 2010), 198.

6. Eugene Peterson, *The Word Made Flesh: The Language of Jesus in His Stories and Prayers* (London: Hodder & Stoughton, 2008), chap. 3.

7. William Shakespeare, *Henry V*, act 4, scene 3. Lin-Manuel Miranda, "The Story of Tonight," *Hamilton: An American Musical*, Atlantic Records, 2015, MP3.

8. Winston Churchill, "Their Finest Hour" speech before the House of Commons, June 18, 1940, WinstonChurchill.org, https://www .winstonchurchill.org/resources/speeches/1940-the-finest-hour /their-finest-hour/.

9. Paul Copan, *Is God a Moral Monster? Making Sense of the Old Testament God* (Grand Rapids: Baker Books, 2011), 172.

10. Copan, *Is God a Moral Monster?*, 171.

11. Joshua Ryan Butler, *The Skeletons in God's Closet* (Nashville: Thomas Nelson, 2014), 228.

12. Enns, *The Bible Tells Me So*, 231 (see intro., n. 2).

13. Nicola Slee, *Praying Like a Woman* (Oxford: SPCK, 2006), 36–37.

14. Butler, *Skeletons in God's Closet*, 243.

15. Scott Arbeiter, "America's Duty to Take in Refugees," *New York Times*, September 23, 2016, https://www.nytimes.com/2016/09/24/opinion /americas-duty-to-take-in-refugees.html.

16. Gregory A. Boyd, *The Crucifixion of the Warrior God* (Minneapolis: Fortress Press, 2017), xxx.

17. Boyd, 1261.

18. Boyd, 701–66.

CHAPTER 4: WISDOM STORIES

1. Alfred Lord Tennyson, cited by William M. Ramsay, *Westminster Guide to the Books of the Bible* (Louisville: Westminster John Knox Press, 1994), 144.

2. Ellen Davis, *Getting Involved with God: Rediscovering the Old Testament* (Plymouth, UK: Cowley Publications, 2001), 122.

3. Beal, *Rise and Fall of the Bible*, 168 (see chap. 1, n. 11).

4. Theodor Adorno, cited in Beal, *Rise and Fall of the Bible*, 163.

5. Christian Smith, *The Bible Made Impossible: Why Biblicism Is Not a Truly Evangelical Reading of Scripture* (Grand Rapids: Brazos Press, 2012), x–xi.

6. Martin Luther and E. Theodore Bachmann, *Luther's Works*, vol. 35, *Word and Sacrament I* (Philadelphia: Fortress, 1960), 362.

7. Beal, *Rise and Fall of the Bible*, 173 (see chap. 1, n. 11).

8. Beal, 27.

9. These are Psalms 100:1; 6:6; 51:3; 22:2; and 89:46.

10. Sebastian Moore, cited by Kathleen Norris, *The Cloister Walk* (New York: Riverhead Books, 1997), 91.

11. Norris, *The Cloister Walk*, 95.

12. Norris, *The Cloister Walk*, 94.

13. Denise Hopkins, *Journey Through the Psalms* (St. Louis: Chalice Press, 2002), 5–6. See also Lester Meyer, "A Lack of Laments in the Church's Use of the Psalter," *Lutheran Quarterly* (Spring 1993): 67–78.

14. Soong-Chan Rah, *Prophetic Lament: A Call to Justice in Troubled Times* (Downers Grove, IL: InterVarsity Press, 2015), 22.

15. Rah, 23.

16. Lynn Hauka, "The Sweetness of Holding Space for Another," *HuffPost: The Blog*, March 28, 2016, https://www.huffingtonpost.com /lynn-hauka/the-sweetness-of-holding-_b_9558266.html.

CHAPTER 5: RESISTANCE STORIES

1. "Thank You, Bree, for Removing the Confederate Flag," Evangelicals for Social Action, June 27, 2015, https://web.archive.org/web/2015090 6121119/http://www.evangelicalsforsocialaction.org/nonviolence-and -peacemaking/thank-you-bree-for-removing-the-confederate-flag-2/.

2. "Bree Newsome Speaks for the First Time After Courageous Act of Civil Disobedience," *Blue Nation Review*, June 29, 2015, http:// archives.bluenationreview.com/exclusive-bree-newsome-speaks-for -the-first-time-after-courageous-act-of-civil-disobedience/.

3. Rob Bell, *What Is the Bible? How an Ancient Library of Poems, Letters, and Stories Can Transform the Way You Think and Feel About Everything* (New York: HarperOne, 2017), 215.

4. Walter Brueggemann, *The Prophetic Imagination*, 2nd ed. (Minneapolis: Fortress, 2001), 6.

5. Brueggemann, 40.

6. "Walter Brueggemann: The Prophetic Imagination," *On Being with Krista Tippett*, Onbeing.org, December 19, 2013, https://onbeing.org /programs/walter-brueggemann-the-prophetic-imagination/.

7. Knight and Levine, *The Meaning of the Bible*, 252 (see chap. 2, n. 9).
8. "Inspired by Martin Luther King Jr., a New Civil Rights Leader Takes Center Stage," *Guardian*, October 25, 2017, https://www.theguardian.com/us-news/2017/oct/25/william-barber-martin-luther-king-jr-civil-rights-leader.
9. Winner, *Still*, 111 (see chap. 2, n. 5).
10. Herodotus, *The Persian Wars*, 3.92.
11. N. T. Wright, *How God Became King: The Forgotten Story of the Gospels* (New York: HarperOne, 2016), 37.

CHAPTER 6: GOSPEL STORIES

1. Flannery O'Connor, *Mystery and Manners* (New York: Farrar, Straus & Giroux, 1969), 96.
2. Quoted in Scot McKnight, *The King Jesus Gospel* (Grand Rapids: Zondervan, 2011), 82.
3. N. T. Wright, *Surprised by Hope: Rethinking Heaven, the Resurrection, and the Mission of the Church* (New York: HarperOne, 2008), 19.
4. Matthew 13:44; 13:33; 13:25; 13:47; and 13:44.
5. Dallas Willard, *The Divine Conspiracy: Recovering Our Hidden Life in God* (New York: HarperCollins, 1998), 41.
6. "Lutheran Minister Preaches a Gospel of Love to Junkies, Drag Queens and Outsiders," NPR, September 17, 2015, https://www.npr.org/templates/transcript/transcript.php?storyId=441139500.
7. Sara Miles, *Take This Bread* (New York: Ballantine, 2008), xiii.
8. Oscar Wilde, *The Importance of Being Earnest and Other Plays* (London: Pan Macmillan, 2017).
9. Amy-Jill Levine, *Short Stories by Jesus* (New York: HarperOne, 2015), 6.
10. Robert Farrar Capon, *Kingdom, Grace, Judgment: Paradox, Outrage, and Vindication in the Parables of Jesus* (Grand Rapids: Eerdmans, 2002), 15.

CHAPTER 7: FISH STORIES

1. Jeffrey John, *The Meaning in the Miracles* (Grand Rapids: Eerdmans, 2001).
2. John, 10.

3. John, 11.

4. Wright, *Surprised by Hope*, 75 (see chap. 6, n. 3).

5. Dallas Willard, *Renovation of the Heart: Putting on the Character of Christ* (Colorado Springs: NavPress, 2002).

6. Shane Claiborne's Facebook page, accessed March 21, 2018, https://www.facebook.com/ShaneClaiborne/posts/10151769308346371.

7. Sara Miles, *Jesus Freak: Feeding, Healing, Raising the Dead* (San Francisco: Jossey-Bass, 2010), 105.

THE LETTER

1. Background for this chapter is drawn from Brian J. Walsh and Sylvia Keesmaat, *Colossians Remixed: Subverting the Empire* (Downers Grove, IL: InterVarsity Press, 2004).

CHAPTER 8: CHURCH STORIES

1. M. Eugene Boring, *An Introduction to the New Testament: History, Literature, Theology* (Louisville: Westminster John Knox Press, 2012), 196.

2. In the ancient world, letters were sometimes composed in the name of a famous teacher from the past, and scholars suspect that, given the language employed and other historical indicators, Ephesians, 1 and 2 Timothy, and Titus were not composed by Paul himself, but by students writing under his name.

3. Adam Hamilton, *Making Sense of the Bible: Rediscovering the Power of Scripture Today* (New York: HarperOne, 2016), 76.

4. Scot McKnight, *The Blue Parakeet: Rethinking How You Read the Bible* (Grand Rapids: Zondervan, 2008), 202.

5. For an in-depth look at what the Bible says about gender and sexuality, see James Brownson, *Bible, Gender, Sexuality* (Grand Rapids: Eerdmans, 2013); and Matthew Vines, *God and the Gay Christian* (New York: Convergent, 2015).

6. Boring, *Introduction to the New Testament*, 205.

7. Enns, *The Bible Tells Me So*, 244 (see intro., no. 2).

8. N. T. Wright, *The New Testament and the People of God* (Minneapolis: Fortress Press, 1992), 6.

9. To learn more about the authorship of the Epistles, start with Hamilton, *Making Sense of the Bible*, 85–90.

10. Stephen J. Binz, *Paul: Apostle to All the Nations* (Grand Rapids: Brazos Press, 2011), 2.

EPILOGUE

1. Gregory Mobley, *The Return of the Chaos Monsters: And Other Backstories of the Bible* (Grand Rapids: Eerdmans, 2012), 7.

2. Wright, *Surprised by Hope*, 208 (see chap. 6, n. 3).

3. Mobley, *Return of the Chaos Monsters*, 6.

4. Daniel J. Siegel and Tina Payne Bryson, *The Whole-Brain Child: 12 Revolutionary Strategies to Nurture Your Child's Developing Mind* (New York: Random House, 2011), 29.

5. Alan Greene, "Why Children Ask 'Why,'" DrGreene.com, March 13, 2000, https://www.drgreene.com/qa-articles/why-children-ask-why/.